Investment Treaty Arbitration
Judging Under Uncertainty

Investment claims have exposed the vague nature of the standards by which arbitral tribunals are expected to adjudicate them and the policy reasons which explicitly or implicitly have an influence. The ad hoc nature of the tribunals and the decisions reached on various controversial issues have brought to the fore the issue of consistency.

Andrés Rigo Sureda's Hersch Lauterpacht Memorial Lectures examine how arbitral discretion is exercised in the face of uncertainty of the law. It explores the choices made by arbitral tribunals as they approach treaty interpretation, as they search for limits in determining jurisdiction and the content of the standards of protection, and as they search for consistency in the exercise of arbitral discretion.

ANDRÉS RIGO SUREDA is a judge on the Administrative Tribunal of the IMF and a member of the Sanctions Committee (the Anticorruption Tribunal) of the Inter-American Development Bank. He has extensive experience as an arbitrator and mediator in commercial and investor–states disputes, and served with the World Bank in various capacities from 1973 to 2000, including Assistant General Counsel and Deputy General Counsel.

Recent books in the Hersch Lauterpacht Memorial Lecture Series

ANDRÉS RIGO SUREDA
Investment Treaty Arbitration:
Judging Under Uncertainty
9781107022515 hardback

RALPH ZACKLIN
The United Nations Secretariat
and the Use of Force in a Unipolar
World: Power v. Principle
9780521194136 hardback

JOHN H. JACKSON
Sovereignty, the WTO, and Changing
Fundamentals of International Law
9780521860079 hardback
9780521748414 paperback

JAN PAULSSON
Denial of Justice in International Law
9780521851183 hardback

FRANCISCO ORREGO VICUNA
International Dispute Settlement in
an Evolving Global Society:
Constitutionalization, Accessibility, Privatization
9780521842396 hardback

MARTTI KOSKENNIEMI
The Gentle Civilizer of Nations:
The Rise and Fall of International Law
1870–1960
9780521623117 hardback
9780521548090 paperback

THOMAS M. FRANCK
Recourse to Force: State Action
against Threats and Armed Attacks
9780521820134 hardback
9780521104203 paperback

ANTONIO CASSESE
Self-Determination of Peoples: A Legal Reappraisal
9780521481878 hardback
9780521637527 paperback

Investment Treaty Arbitration

Judging Under Uncertainty

ANDRÉS RIGO SUREDA

CAMBRIDGE
UNIVERSITY PRESS

CAMBRIDGE UNIVERSITY PRESS
Cambridge, New York, Melbourne, Madrid, Cape Town,
Singapore, São Paulo, Delhi, Tokyo, Mexico City

Cambridge University Press
The Edinburgh Building, Cambridge CB2 8RU, UK

Published in the United States of America by
Cambridge University Press, New York

www.cambridge.org
Information on this title: www.cambridge.org/9781107022515

First published 2012

A catalogue record for this publication is available from the British Library

Library of Congress Cataloguing in Publication data

Rigo Sureda, Andrés
Investment treaty arbitration : judging under uncertainty / Andres Rigo Sureda.
p. cm.
Includes bibliographical references and index.
ISBN 978-1-107-02251-5 (hardback : alk. paper)
1. Investments, Foreign – Law and legislation. 2. Arbitration and award,
International. 3. Commercial treaties. I. Title.
K3830.R54 2012
346′.092 – dc23 2012009121

ISBN 978-1-107-02251-5 Hardback

Contents

Foreword

by Sir Elihu Lauterpacht C.B.E. Q.C. LL.D.

In the remarkable substantive and procedural expansion of international law during the last half-century the development and protection of international investment has occupied a prominent position. And within this area a significant contribution has come from the impressive growth in the international litigation that is one of the principal reflections of the enhanced status of individuals and corporations in the international legal system. In the forefront has been the adoption in 1965 of the International Convention on the Settlement of Investment Disputes, together with the emergence of hundreds of bilateral treaties containing watertight provisions for the settlement of such disputes. The present thoughtful and incisive book identifies and probes many of the problems now embedded in the extensive arbitral jurisprudence reflecting this development. They have deep significance for international law.

Nobody could be better qualified to explore these matters than the present author, Dr Andrés Rigo Sureda. For more than twenty-five years he occupied a central position in this field as one of the leading lawyers of the World Bank, eventually becoming its Deputy General Counsel. Since leaving the Bank he has himself been an active practitioner and arbitrator in the field. His connection with Cambridge goes back to 1968 when he was a Ph.D. student on an Overseas Research Fellowship of the BIICL and later a Senior Rouse Bell Student of Trinity College. We remain grateful to him for contributing this stimulating study, originally given as a series of Hersch Lauterpacht Memorial Lectures, containing much enlightening discussion of perennial problems of international adjudication, not the least of which is his penetrating treatment of the role and limits of judicial discretion.

E. Lauterpacht
June 2011

Acknowledgements

This study has its origin in the Sir Hersch Lauterpacht Memorial Lectures delivered at the Lauterpacht Centre of Cambridge University in late 2008. The author thanks Professors Sir Eli Lauterpacht and James Crawford for their invitation to deliver the lectures on the 25th anniversary of the Lauterpacht Centre. The author is grateful to the Warden and Fellows of All Souls College who elected him to a visiting fellowship (2006–7) to carry out research for the Lectures. Thanks are also due to Judd Kessler and Professors Michael W. Riesman and Edith Brown-Weiss, who read the manuscript and made useful suggestions. The enthusiastic and thorough editing of an earlier draft by Federica Paddeu, a Cambridge graduate student, is particularly recognized. Any remaining infelicitous language or errors are the author's alone.

Table of cases

By alphabetical order of claimant. The decisions and awards listed are generally available at http://ita.law.uvic.ca/. In some instances they are not, and can be found in the source indicated.

Introduction

The international law of investments has been an area of exponential growth in the last two decades. This development is sustained by two pillars: first, bilateral or multilateral treaties of promotion and protection of investments (BITs) and second, the International Convention on the Settlement of Investment Disputes (ICSID) Convention.

The first BIT is reputed to have been signed in 1959 between Germany and Pakistan. Since then, BITs in excess of 2,700 have been concluded. Although the first such agreements pre-date the debates in the United Nations (UN) on the New International Economic Order, it was precisely in response to the debates in the General Assembly concerning the measure of compensation owed in case of expropriation that the negotiation of BITs started in earnest, first and foremost with the objective to provide prompt, adequate and effective compensation.

The United Kingdom (UK) concluded the first BIT in 1975; the United States launched a BIT programme in 1977. A main feature of BITs is the offer made by the State to investors to arbitrate disputes related to their investments. BITs respond to a liberal doctrine of increased prosperity through foreign investment. They are symbolic of the wave of privatizations and free movement of capital of the last three decades. As investments have soured and cases against States have multiplied, the mood in some countries seems to be changing and new generations of BITs have been more restrictive, as witnessed by the new US model BIT.[1] It is too early to gauge what the effect of the recent financial crisis will be, in particular since

[1] US Model BIT (2004), available at: http://ustraderep.gov/Trade_Sectors/Investment/Model_BIT/Section_Index.html.

it puts into question the consensus on the role of the State in economic matters prevalent in the last three decades.

The ICSID Convention was signed in 1965 and entered into force in 1966.[2] The drafting and negotiation of the Convention was sponsored by the World Bank – to which ICSID is affiliated – which adopted the initiative of creating the Centre for the sole purpose of administering legal disputes between investors and States arising out of investments. The World Bank's initiative was prompted by the concern that political risks could deter the flow of foreign private capital to developing countries.[3] The submission of disputes to third party settlement was seen as a way to de-politicize them: as a counterpoint to the host State's agreement to third party settlement, the national State of the investor agrees not to pursue the diplomatic protection of the investor, except in cases of non-compliance with the award.

De-politicization of investment disputes through judicial settlement confirms Hersch Lauterpacht's thesis that the characterization of a dispute as a political or legal one is an invalid distinction under international law. Lauterpacht drew attention to the fact that 'disputes of high political importance were submitted to, and settled by, a purely judicial process' and that 'disputes obviously capable of decision on strictly legal lines were withheld from that procedure, on the ground that they were essentially political in their nature'.[4] Thus a dispute may be legal or political, even if capable of a legal decision. He drew the conclusion that 'it is the refusal of the State to submit the dispute to judicial settlement, and not the intrinsic nature of the controversy, which makes it political'.[5] However, when by definition one of the parties is a State and disputes concern matters of State policy and regulation, the political context is never far away.

The prohibition of recourse to diplomatic protection in ICSID cases and the fact that more often than not exhaustion of local remedies is not required before recourse to arbitration under investment treaties results in the elimination of two filters – one juridical, another political – before a dispute reaches the international arbitration stage and helps explain the growth of investment treaty arbitration. In any case, the rush of private

[2] Convention on the Settlement of Investment Disputes between States and Nationals of Other States, 18 March 1965, in force 14 October 1966, 575 UNTS 159.

[3] A. Broches, *Selected Essays: World Bank, ICSID, and other Subjects of Public and Private International Law* (Dordrecht: Nijhoff, 1995), 193.

[4] H. Lauterpacht, *The Function of Law in the International Community* (Oxford: Clarendon Press, 1933), 163. See also, B. Stern, 'Are Some Issues Too Political to Be Arbitrable?' *ICSID Review* 24 (2009) 90.

[5] Ibid., 164.

claims against States, even if large in historical terms, is not so in relation to the amount of foreign investment flows during the last decades.[6] The surge of private party claims against States in the era of investment treaties should not be surprising. Hersch Lauterpacht observed that the origin of most international claims lies in injuries suffered by private parties, and recounted all the cases before the Permanent Court of International Justice (PCIJ) which had originated in injuries to private parties by the respondent State.[7]

The BITs clauses on which most of these claims are based have exposed the vague nature of the standards by which arbitral tribunals are expected to adjudicate the claims, the resulting discretion of the tribunals among a variety of legally justified outcomes and the policy reasons which explicitly or implicitly have inclined a tribunal in favour of one or the other. The *ad hoc* nature of the tribunals and the variety of decisions on controversial issues has brought to the fore issues of consistency and how to solve them. The subject of this monograph is how in the face of uncertainty discretion is exercised. Part I focuses generally on judicial discretion, and more particularly on the choices made by arbitral tribunals as they approach treaty interpretation. Part II is devoted to the search for limits in determining jurisdiction and the content of the standards of protection, and Part III deals with principles, precedents and publicists and the extent to which they may assist in the search for consistency in the exercise of arbitral tribunal discretion.

[6] W. Michael Reisman, 'International Investment Arbitration and ADR: Married but Best Living Apart' *ICSID Review* 24 (2009) 186–7.

[7] 'Apart from territorial disputes, the great majority of cases of international judicial and arbitral settlement arise out of alleged infractions of private interests – a not untimely reminder that although international law is a law primarily between States, it regulates and protects the interests of the individual, who is the ultimate unit of the law of nations, as indeed of all law. For this reason the private nature of the claim underlying the dispute is not decisive as to its importance for general international law', in H. Lauterpacht, *The Development of International Law by the International Court* (London: Stevens, 1958), 31–2.

Part I

Discretion: the search for meaning

1

Uncertainty, judicial discretion and policy

Writing about the work of the International Court of Justice (ICJ), Hersch Lauterpacht pointed to the difficulty of judging between contentions which may deserve equal recognition:

[I]t is seldom a question of a clear and undisputed right against the entire absence of a right. It is, as a rule, a question of giving effect to a better right against a right of less compelling merit.[1]

How is the better right determined? He continues:

It is that necessity of making a decision not between claims which are fully justified and claims which have no foundation at all but between claims which have varying degrees of legal merit – it is that necessity which, in common with the activity of legal tribunals generally, characterizes the work of the International Court . . . [M]any a case decided by the Court would not necessarily have given the impression of a manifestly wrong application of the law if the decision had gone the other way . . . It would provide an exercise of some interest and instruction to survey the work of the Court from that point of view.[2]

I found inspiration in these reflections to choose the subject of the lectures on which this monograph is based and thus honour the publication of *The Function of Law in the International Community* seventy-five years ago.

What criteria are used to measure the 'varying degrees of legal merit' of claims? If the Court could decide otherwise without 'a manifestly wrong

[1] H. Lauterpacht, *Development of International Law by the International Court, being a revised edition of The Development of International Law by the Permanent Court of International Justice* (London: Stevens, 1958), 396–7.

[2] Ibid., 398.

application of the law', on what basis does it decide between two acceptable alternatives from a legal point of view? To answer these questions is to determine how judges use their discretion and what policy arguments underlie their choices, whether or not acknowledged by them. These issues are not confined to the ICJ or to international law. They are common to adjudication under any legal system.

A student of judicial discretion, Judge Barak of Israel's Supreme Court has defined it as a normative concept which 'reflects a state of affairs in which a judge must choose among a number of options, none of which the legal system has determined to be the right choice'.[3] At the level of the ICJ, Judge Bedjaoui, writing extrajudicially, speaks about the *opportunité*[4] of decisions:

> [l]orsque la norme juridique ouvre au juge le choix entre deux ou plusieurs solutions, toutes légales par consequent, elle l'investit d'une latitude ou d'une liberté de décision, ce qui lui confère un pouvoir dit discrétionnaire. Grâce à cette liberté, bien encandré par la légalité, le juge tente de prendre *la décision la plus opportune possible*.[5]

The root causes of judicial discretion may be as varied as the nature of the legal system itself: the limitations of language, inability to predict the future, lack of knowledge of a certain field in the course of its development, or lack of agreement on more specific terms. Thus, for instance, Koskenniemi attributes this situation to the reversibility of legal argument:

> Reversibility results from the way our legal concepts need to conserve both projects, both conceptual schemes within themselves. For if it were the case that concepts which preferred either community or autonomy would always be preferred, then legal argument would be pointless. Merely to state the dispute would be to state the correct solution . . . In some way all legal arguments used in above examples are valid legal arguments and the issue seems to be only to decide a relative preference between them. But such preference becomes impossible because the initially opposing arguments come to look indistinguishable. Because each legal

[3] A. Barak, *Purposive Interpretation in Law* (Princeton University Press, 2005), 208.

[4] 'Le pouvoir discrétionaire du juge international, et son corollaire épisodique de circonstance, l'opportunité, appartiennent nécessairement à la fonction judiciaire comme l'ombre à l'homme': M. Bedjaoui, 'L'opportunité dans les decisions de la Cour Internationale de Justice' in Laurence Boisson de Chazournes and Vera Gowlland-Debbas (eds.), *The International Legal System in Quest of Equity and Universality: Liber Amicorum Georges Abi-Saab* (The Hague: Martinus Nijhoff Publishers, 2001), 589.

[5] 'Ce serait un absurde défi du législateur d'exiger du juge international la stricte application d'une norme dont il ne lui a pas rigoureusement déterminé le contenu'. Ibid., 575.

concept can and must be argued from an ascending as well as a descending perspective the sole criterion for making a preference is lost.[6]

The area of discretion left to courts and tribunals is related to the generality and vagueness of the law to be applied. The more abstract or general the terms of the norm, the greater the discretion effectively delegated by the legislature or by treaty parties to those tribunals that in the future may interpret them.[7] Several causes might underlie such generality or vagueness: States may not have been able to agree on the definition of a term, they may have opted to provide for standards of conduct rather than clear-cut rules, they may have intentionally left a certain provision open for future development, or else the field in question may not be sufficiently developed in general.

Discretion is more acutely relevant in international law. Elihu Lauterpacht observes that the uncertainty concerning how international law comes into being is part of the intellectual excitement of the study of international law: 'today's rule reflects in part yesterday's deviance; and . . . the cloth of obligation is partly cut from the pattern of non-conformity'.[8] The imprecision and the scarcity of substantive rules translate into more significant judicial freedom of determination.[9]

Investment treaties themselves are indeterminate to the extent that they provide standards of compliance, the content of which is left to be specified by arbitral tribunals.[10] This development has parallels in domestic law and

6 M. Koskenniemi, *From Apology to Utopia* (Cambridge University Press, 2005), 506 (original emphasis removed).

7 '. . . le pouvoir discretionnaire se nourrit du vague d'une norme juridique'. Bedjaoui, 'L' opportunité', 574.

8 E. Lauterpacht, 'The Development of the Law of International Organization by the Decisions of International Tribunals' *Recueil des cours* 152 (1976) 4 377–478 at 389. 'Le processus de création de règles en droit international fait que les normes y jouissent d'une très grande relativité et que celles qui se rapprochent le plus du statut de règles universelles sont souvent ambigues': J. Salmon, 'Quelques observations sur la qualification en droit international public' in C. Perelman and P. Foriers (eds.), *La motivation des décisions de justice* (Brussels: Bruylant, 1978), 348. 'Bien souvent les contradictions existantes au moment de la création de la règle de droit international n'ont pas été résolues ou ont eté mises entre parenthèses. Elles demeurent. Le droit international affectionne les formules ambigues qui ne résolvent qu'à moitié les choses': ibid., 350.

9 Lauterpacht, 'The Development of the Law', 395.

10 'Le contenu des traités est souvent très imprécis . . . les traités recourent très fréquemment à la technique du standard: standard du traitement juste et équitable et de la pleine et entière protection par example dans les traités relatifs aux investissements. Cette technique qui exclut l'indication d'obligations précises se réfère à un seuil de comportement dont le contenu ne pourra être apprécié par le juge qu'au cas par cas au regard des situations concrètes présentées devant lui. Dans cette technique, les États s'abstiennent

in the field of human rights. In the case of investment treaties, the States commit themselves, for instance, to fair and equitable treatment of investors and their investments, to provide them with full protection and security, and not to take measures, without compensation, that may be tantamount to expropriation.[11] The resulting discretion points to the importance of policy in the decisions of arbitral tribunals. As a general matter, Friedmann drew attention to the unavoidable role of policy in judicial decision making:

> The policy element in the judicial decision may be refined; it may be pushed back further and further; the area of uncertainty may be reduced. But there must always remain a point at which a choice has to be made, and it is necessary to determine the factors guiding that choice.[12]

This is even more the case in investment arbitration where the area of uncertainty remains large, and consequently the significance of the reasons for the choice made among possible outcomes:

> The justification of the decision must depend upon the reasoned assessment of the relative, or comparative, desirability and undesirability of the consequences which

délibérément d'exercer leur role normatif et se reposent sur le juge ou l'arbitre du soin de concrétiser le contenu des obligations': G. Burdeau, 'Le pouvoir créateur de la jurisprudence internationale à l'épreuve de la dispersion des juridictions' *Archives de philosophie du droit* 50 (2007) 289, 297.

11 'The contrast between rules and standards identifies the fact that with some legal provisions, interpreters have to do a great deal of work in order to give law real content. The meaning of a standard depends on what happens when it is applied, and those who decide what happens are likely to proceed casuistically. Of course casuistical judgments may well generate categories that provide great guidance for the future', C.R. Sunstein, *Legal Reasoning and Political Conflict* (New York: Oxford University Press, 1996), 27. 'It is in justifying the value-judgments which are made in these various situations of judicial discretion that policy arguments are used. By relying on the justifications for new rules, or interpretations of discretionary standards, the judges seek to persuade the legal audience of the rightness of their decision, and to show that they have made a legitimate exercise of the political power entrusted to them': J. Bell, *Policy Arguments in Judicial Decisions* (Oxford: Clarendon Press, 1983), 29–30.

12 W. Friedmann, 'Legal Philosophy and Judicial Lawmaking' *Colum L. R.* 61 (1961) 821, 826. See also MacCormick, for whom '[w]hen a question is finely balanced, as the question here was and when either answer can be given consistently with the words used in the Act [he is speaking of statutory interpretation], a ruling must be made for one or the other; that ruling, to be justified, must show it to be the more acceptable given a consistent and principled "theory" . . . our answer must depend upon the values we bring to bear on the question', in N. MacCormick, *Legal Reasoning and Legal Theory* (Oxford: Clarendon Press, 1978), 212–13. He continues: 'But there is another theory by reference to which the other is right, and to have reasoned grounds for saying that one theory as against the other is right, we should require a third, higher-order, theory, which might in turn be challenged by a fourth – and so on. Short of an infinite regress we must make, and live with, our own choices . . . ', at 213.

the decision as a decision of principle will entail. But it can only fall within the judges' rather than the legislature's province to make such evaluations and give effect to them if there exist within the law competing analogies or general rules or principles such that the decision – whichever way made – can be shown to be supported by the existing law even though it be not compelled one way or the other by an unequivocal rule of mandatory character.[13]

Justifications can provide guidance for the future and assist in developing an influential jurisprudence;[14] to guide future tribunals, a judgment must be seen to have a firm grounding in principle, which in turn makes it jurisprudentially significant by virtue of what has been termed 'the law behind the case'.[15] The reasons provided by arbitrators depend on how they envision the role of policy arguments in making choices.

Tribunals may believe in judicial restraint where considerations of policy have no place, or else they may consider as illusory the notion that legal rules may be applied without considerations of policy. Tribunals which adhere to the first alternative consider that they should apply law as it exists and apply it strictly. In case of doubt, a tribunal predicating judicial restraint will most likely consider that the matter is not covered by the law. If the law is unsatisfactory, it is for the legislature to redress it. It is 'common to find supporters of restraint admitting that a particular decision is regrettable, while at the same time holding it to be inevitable on the ground that the law leaves no room for choice'.[16] On the other hand, in doubtful cases, judicial activists will first decide if the case should be covered and then construe the rule accordingly. It is 'the judge's job to produce an appropriate result if at all possible, elements which others think conclusive are treated as simply factors in the equation'.[17]

Statements about the adjudicatory policy followed by a particular arbitral tribunal are not uncommon,[18] but it may be more revealing to look into what a tribunal does than what it says. In *Renta*, the Tribunal warned that

[13] Ibid., 173.
[14] J.G. Merrils, *The Development of International Law by the European Court of Human Rights* (2nd edn, Manchester University Press, 1993), 34.
[15] Ibid., 21, quoting Lauterpacht, *Development of International Law*, 71.
[16] Ibid., 231. [17] Ibid., 232.
[18] See, for instance, *Glamis Gold, Ltd.* v. *The United States of America*, UNCITRAL Award, 8 June 2009, paras. 3–9, available at: www.state.gov/s/l/c10986.htm; and *Saipem S.p.A.* v. *The People's Republic of Bangladesh*, ICSID Case No. ARB/05/07, Award, 30 June 2009, para. 90, for a statement of policy in respect of precedents.

'speculations as to policy desiderata' in favour of one reading or another of an instrument should be considered with care:[19]

> To choose one of the contending policy theses as the reason to read a BIT in a particular way may be presumptuous. The stakes are high and the policy decisions appertain to the State-parties to the treaties. Speculations relied upon as the basis of purposive readings of a text run the risk of encroachment upon fundamental policy determinations. The same is true when 'confirmation' of hypothetical intentions is said to be found in considerations external to the text. The duty of the Tribunal is to discover and not to create meaning.[20]

The discovery of meaning, the discovery of the law rather than its creation, is a traditional fiction cloaking the role of judges. According to this fiction, law is resting on an imaginary shelf merely waiting for the judges to find it. However, the distinction between discovery and creation may not in practice be easily drawn. The same tribunal had no difficulty in affirming that '[i]t cannot seriously be thought that investors would be attracted by a regime that gave them access to international arbitration of the issue of the quantum of compensation but not of whether any compensation is due at all'.[21]

Some arbitral tribunals may defer to the policy role of the States in setting limits to which transactions may qualify as investments for purposes of their consent to arbitration. For instance, any State may exclude investments below certain limits, 'But other States may precisely want to benefit from the aggregate investment flows of attracting the small to middle sized business which have contributed so notably to the development of economies . . . This is *their* policy choice; not that of ICSID arbitrators.'[22] On the other hand, other tribunals may limit investments below certain monetary limits without acknowledgement that they may be stepping into a role best reserved to the parties of the investment treaty concerned.[23] This may be the result of caution in one case and lack of awareness of the policy role being played by the tribunal in the other.

The first time a North American Free Trade Agreement (NAFTA) arbitral tribunal considered a petition for *amicus curiae* in an arbitration conducted under the United Nations Common International Trade Law

[19] *Renta 4 S.VS.A et al.* v. *Russian Federation*, SCC No. 24/2007, Award on Preliminary Objections, 20 March 2009, para. 92, available at: http://ita.law.uvic.ca/documents/Renta.pdf.

[20] Ibid., para. 93. [21] Ibid., para. 52.

[22] *Pantechniki SA Contractors & Engineers* v. *Republic of Albania*, para. 45. Emphasis in original.

[23] *Malaysian Historical Salvors, SDN, BHD* v. *Malaysia*, paras. 130ff.

(UNCITRAL) Arbitration Rules – the *Methanex* case – the Tribunal noted that 'there is nothing in either the UNCITRAL Arbitration Rules or Chapter 11, Section B, that either expressly confers upon the Tribunal the power to accept *amicus* submissions or expressly provides that the Tribunal shall have no such power'.[24] In use of the discretion afforded by these provisions, the Tribunal decided that it had the power to accept *amicus* submissions because of public interest and because 'the Chapter 11 arbitral process could benefit from being perceived as more open or transparent; or conversely be harmed if seen as unduly secretive'.[25] Notwithstanding the fact that this was a first in investment treaty arbitration and it would have repercussions for future cases, the *Methanex* tribunal considered of lesser importance 'the factor raised by the Claimant as to the danger of setting a precedent'. In the Tribunal's view:

> It ha[d] no power to determine for other arbitration tribunals how to interpret Article 15(1) [of the UNCITRAL Arbitration Rules]; and in a later arbitration, there may be other circumstances leading that tribunal to exercise its discretion differently. For each arbitration, the decision must be made by its tribunal in the particular circumstances of the arbitration only.[26]

The Tribunal adopted a position which is correct from a formal point of view as regards the lack of doctrine of binding precedent in international law, but it contrasts with its willingness to consider the consequences of its decision in favour of a policy of more transparent arbitration proceedings. The Tribunal was making an important policy decision for the future of investment treaty arbitration but, at the same time, it was reluctant to recognize that by so doing its role in fact went beyond deciding the issue for the instant case.

Caution may take other forms. A tribunal may dissociate itself from the law which it is required to apply. Lord Devlin considered it 'useful for the judge to be able to dissociate himself from the law, to hint to the litigant that he would prefer to decide otherwise, but is bound by the law'.[27] The *Loewen* Tribunal found that: 'By any standard of measurement, the trial involving O'Keefe and Loewen was a disgrace. By any standard of review, the tactics of O'Keefe's lawyers, particularly Mr. Gary, were impermissible. By any standard of evaluation, the trial judge failed to afford Loewen the

[24] *Methanex* v. *United States*, UNCITRAL (NAFTA), Decision on Petitions from Third Persons to Intervene as 'Amici Curiae', 15 January 2001, 7 ICSID Reports 224, para. 24.
[25] Ibid., para. 49. [26] Ibid., para. 51.
[27] Quoted in P. Atiyah, 'Judges and Policy' *Israel L. Rev.* 15 (1980) 346, at 362.

process that was due.'[28] Nonetheless the Tribunal dismissed the claim on a questionable application of the exhaustion of the local remedies rule and the continuous nationality rule, and by piercing the corporate veil while denying that it was doing so. In light of the law thus found, the Tribunal felt compelled to add the following conclusion by way of apology[29] for its decision:

We think it right to add one final word. A reader following our account of the injustices which were suffered by Loewen and Mr. Raymond Loewen in the Courts of Mississippi could well be troubled to find that they emerge from the present long and costly proceedings with no remedy at all. After all, we have held that judicial wrongs may in principle be brought home to the State Party under Chapter Eleven, and have criticized the Mississippi proceedings in the strongest terms. There was unfairness here towards the foreign investor. Why not use the weapons at hand to put it right? What clearer case than the present could there be for the ideals of NAFTA to be given some teeth?

This human reaction has been present in our minds throughout but we must be on guard against allowing it to control our decision. Far from fulfilling the purposes of NAFTA, an intervention on our part would compromise them by obscuring the crucial separation between the international obligations of the State under NAFTA, of which the fair treatment of foreign investors in the judicial sphere is but one aspect, and the much broader domestic responsibilities of every nation towards litigants of whatever origin who appear before its national courts. Subject to explicit international agreement permitting external control or review, these latter responsibilities are for each individual state to regulate according to its own chosen appreciation of the ends of justice. As we have sought to make clear, we find nothing in NAFTA to justify the exercise by this Tribunal of an appellate function parallel to that which belongs to the courts of the host nation. In the last resort, a failure by that nation to provide adequate means of remedy may amount to an international wrong but only in the last resort. The line may be hard to draw, but it is real. Too great a readiness to step from outside into the domestic arena, attributing the shape of an international wrong to what is really a local error (however serious), will damage both the integrity of the domestic judicial system and the viability of NAFTA itself. The natural instinct, when someone observes a miscarriage of justice, is to step in and try to put it right, but the interests of the

[28] *Loewen Group, Inc. and Raymond L. Loewen* v. *United States*, ICSID Case No. ARB(AF)/98/3 (NAFTA), Award, 26 June 2003, 7 ICSID Reports 442, para. 119.

[29] N. Rubins, '*Loewen v United States*: The Burial of an Investor-State Arbitration Claim' *Arbitration International* 21 (2005) 1, 6. Mr. Rubins was part of the legal team of the claimant.

international investing community demand that we must observe the principles which we have been appointed to apply, and stay our hands.[30]

From the time the award was rendered, the grounds for dismissal of the *Loewen* claim have been attributed to political factors, namely, to avoid a decision against the United States and its possible effect on NAFTA. This has since been confirmed by the US-appointed arbitrator, Judge Abner Mikva, who in an unusually candid address disclosed that *after*[31] he agreed to serve on the arbitral tribunal and before the tribunal was constituted he met with the officials of the Department of Justice of the United States. These officials told him: 'You know, judge, if we lose this case we could lose NAFTA.' He replied: 'Well, if you want to put pressure on me, then that does it.'[32] Thus, in this case the detachment of the Tribunal from a doubtful understanding of the law seems to be the result of barter among Tribunal members in order to ensure that the United States would not lose the case: '[Judge Mikva] going along with that conclusion of judicial impropriety in exchange for a curious technical trump card which secured an ultimate "triumph" for the U.S.'.[33]

The *Mihaly* Tribunal accepted an objection to its jurisdiction *rationae materiae* because in the circumstances of the case pre-investment expenditures did not qualify as an investment. Although the Tribunal considered that it was not required to express an opinion on the remedies open to a party in the claimant's situation, it nonetheless went on to give just such an opinion:

... during periods of lengthy negotiations even absent any contractual relationships obligations may arise such as the obligation to conduct the negotiations in good faith. These obligations if breached may entitle the innocent party to damages, or some other remedy. However, these remedies do not arise because an investment had been made, but rather because the requirements of proper conduct in relation to negotiation for an investment may have been breached. That

[30] *Loewen*, Award, 70–1, paras. 241–2. [31] Emphasis added.

[32] Quoted in D. Schneiderman, 'Judicial Politics and International Investment Arbitration: Seeking an Explanation for Conflicting Outcomes,' 15. Available at: http://works.bepress.com/david_schneiderman/1. Judge Mikva further disclosed that he had been 'on the dissenting side of a difficult problem' since his fellow arbitrators were intent on finding for Loewen. Ibid.

[33] J. Paulsson, 'Moral Hazard in International Dispute Resolution', 7, available at: www.arbitration-icca.org/media/0/12773749999020/paulsson_moral_hazard.pdf.

type of claim is not one to which the Convention has anything to say. They are not arbitrable as a consequence of the Convention.[34]

It is debatable whether the ICSID Convention has nothing to say on this matter. The separate concurring opinion of one of the arbitrators supported joining to the merits the objection to jurisdiction and calling for evidence of international legal and utility precedents and practice,[35] including whether the exculpatory language in the letters exchanged between the parties was designed to ensure that:

there was no contractual liability before a final BOT [Build, Operate, Transfer] contract was signed or whether its effect under Sri Lankan and general principles of international law was to exclude any liability of Sri Lanka arising from its conduct after the award of the Letter of Intent – including a duty to negotiate in good faith.[36]

This would have been a prudent course of action, given that negotiations were incident to making the investment and that the failure of the negotiations was due to the government's insistence that the investor engage in illegal conduct. To compensate for dismissing the claim, the majority explained the remedies open to the claimant after 'blaming' the ICSID Convention for its decision and thus disengaging from the extant law.

The extent of the arbitrators' policy role may not be acknowledged because of reluctance to admit it, or by implicitly denying that arbitrators would have such a role. This is understandable for *ad hoc* temporary tribunals, but whether or not these tribunals acknowledge them, the policy choices are there to be made. If tribunals shy away from this role, whether by denying it or pretending that they are not playing it, there is legitimate cause to pose the question whether:

the tribunal will choose more wisely if it chooses in consciousness of its responsibility rather than in the belief that it has no choice open. This is a question on which there may be divergent views even in the municipal administration of justice. And it must be acknowledged at the very outset that the case for continuing to 'make-believe' that the field of judicial freedom does not exist is very strong on the international level – much stronger certainly than on the municipal level.[37]

[34] *Mihaly International Corporation* v. *Democratic Socialist Republic of Sri Lanka*, ICSID Case No. ARB/00/2, Award, 15 March 2002, 6 ICSID Reports 310, para. 51.
[35] Ibid., 323, para. 6. [36] Ibid.
[37] J. Stone, 'Fictitional Elements in Treaty Interpretation – A Study in the International Judicial Process' *Sydney Law Review* 1(3) (1954) 344, 367.

It is paradoxical that at the international level, where the '*opportunité*' and need for judicial discretion may be higher for the reasons already explained,[38] the reluctance to admit the creative role of the judge is more pronounced than at the municipal level. While this reluctance at the international level may serve the purpose of protecting the growing international judiciary,[39] other factors might explain the persistence of similar reluctance in certain mature municipal systems. In England, the judiciary's belief that 'it is best not to be too explicit about the true nature of the judicial role' has a long historical tradition behind it.[40] Judge Lauterpacht observed in general terms that:

> It is not [the courts'] function deliberately to change the law so as to make it conform with their own views of justice and expediency. This does not mean that they do not in fact shape or even alter the law. *But they do it without admitting it*; they do it while guided at the same time by existing law; they do it while remembering that stability and uncertainty are no less of the essence of the law than justice; they do it, in a word, with caution. The same considerations apply to the administration of international justice.[41]

The same restraint should be shown by arbitral tribunals as a matter of judicial policy in respect of unnecessary arguments for the decision of a particular case on controversial points of law. These may increase uncertainty as to the meaning of the applicable law, breach principles of judicial economy and ignore the merits of silence in adjudication. Silence 'can help minimize conflict, allow the present to learn from the future, and save a great deal of time and expense. In law, as elsewhere, what is said is no more important than what is left unsaid.'[42]

Restraint from contributing to controversial points of law with statements not required to decide the case at hand would seem eminently appropriate to the *ad hoc* nature of investment treaty arbitration. The *Glamis* Tribunal observed that:

[38] Judge Lauterpacht observed that 'the necessity for bold judicial action is particularly great in the international sphere, i.e. in a system of law in which legislative opportunities for modifying rigid, unjust and obsolete rules are somewhat nominal. The result of the clash of these conflicting tendencies is not without interest. It shows itself in both the tendency to caution and the apparent desire to create the appearance of caution', Lauterpacht, *Development of International Law*, 77.

[39] '[T]he fictions which combine to conceal judicial creativeness in international law serve the proper social function of protecting the growing judicial arm against premature strains . . . ' Stone, 'Fictional Elements in Treaty Interpretation', 367.

[40] Atiyah, 'Judges and Policy', 361–2.

[41] Lauterpacht, *Development of International Law*, 75 (emphasis in original).

[42] Sunstein, *Legal Reasoning and Political Conflict*, 39.

a few awards have made statements not required by the case before it. The Tribunal does not agree with this tendency; it believes that its case-specific mandate and the respect demanded for the difficult task faced squarely by some future tribunal instead argues for it to confine its decision to the issues presented.[43]

The Tribunal in *RosInvestCo UK Ltd* v. *The Russian Federation* refrained from entering into the controversy about the interpretation of Most-Favoured-Nation (MFN) clauses:

Therefore, without entering into the much more general question whether MFN-clauses can be used to transfer arbitration clauses from one treaty to another, the Tribunal concludes that, for the specific wording in Article 3(1) of the UK-Soviet BIT, and for the specific purpose of arbitration with regard to expropriation, the wide wording of Article 8 of the Denmark-Russia BIT is not applicable.[44]

More common are examples of the opposite practice. Arbitrators in the *Société Ouest Africaine des Bétons Industriels (SOABI)* v. *State of Senegal* case appended an opinion and a declaration to the final award addressing criticism of their earlier decision on jurisdiction by reviewers of that decision.[45] In *Plama* v. *Bulgaria*, the Tribunal advocated a presumption against an MFN provision incorporating 'by reference dispute settlement provisions in whole or in part set forth in another treaty',[46] despite the fact that this statement was unnecessary for the Tribunal's decision and hence *obiter dicta*.[47] The Annulment Committee in *CMS* v. *Argentina*, in spite of the admitted limitations upon its powers to review the Tribunal's award, concluded that the award contained manifest errors of law and suffered from lacunae and

[43] *Glamis Gold* v. *United States*, para. 8. However, the Tribunal considers that: '[t]he ultimate integrity of the Chapter 11 system as a whole requires a modicum of awareness of each of these tribunals for each other and the system as a whole. The fact that any particular tribunal need not live with the challenge of applying its reasoning in the case before it to a host of different future disputes (the challenge faced by standing adjudicative bodies) does not mean such a tribunal can ignore that challenge. A case-specific mandate is not license to ignore systemic implications. To the contrary, it arguably makes it all the more important that each tribunal renders its case-specific decision with sensitivity to the position of future tribunals and an awareness of other systemic implications', paras. 5–6.

[44] *RosInvestCo UK Ltd.* v. *The Russian Federation*, SCC Case No. Arb. V079/2005, Award on Jurisdiction, October 2007, para. 129, available at: http://ita.law.uvic.ca/documents/RosInvestjurisdiction_decision_2007_10_001.pdf.

[45] *Société Ouest Africaine des Bétons Industriels (SOABI)* v. *State of Senegal*, ICSID Case No. ARB/82/1, Dissenting Opinion, 25 February 1988, 2 ICSID Reports 277; and Declaration of the President of the Tribunal, 25 February 1988, 2 ICSID Reports 333.

[46] *Plama Consortium Limited* v. *Bulgaria*, ICSID Case No. ARB/03/24, Decision on Jurisdiction, 8 February 2005, 13 ICSID Reports 272, para. 223.

[47] See *Renta*, para. 95 and Chapter 5 below for a discussion on precedent and *obiter dicta*.

elisions, nevertheless letting the award stand (with the exception of the umbrella clause) because it could not substitute its own view of the law and its own appreciation of the facts for those of the Tribunal.[48]

Restraint would seem the wiser choice for *ad hoc* tribunals of limited jurisdiction. Avoidance of unnecessary pronouncements on contentious issues would help reduce the perception of a ruptured international investment legal regime and the resulting uncertainty. An international adjudicator deals with a dispute with the objective of contributing to the pacification and normalization of relations between the parties; its decision should not be counterproductive and exacerbate the differences.[49]

[48] *CMS Gas Transmission Company* v. *Argentine Republic*, ICSID Case No. ARB/01/8. Decision on Annulment, 25 September 2007, 14 ICSID Reports 251, para. 158.

[49] 'Sa décision de "dire le droit" ne doit pas être contreproductive et exarceber les passions', M. Bedjaoui, 'L'opportunité dans les décisions de la Cour Internationale de Justice', in Boisson de Chazournes and Gowlland-Debbas (eds.), *The International Legal System in Quest of Equity and Universality*, 588–9.

2

Treaty interpretation

Arbitral tribunals rarely justify their interpretative approach,[1] instead, they start their task of interpreting investment treaties by referring to Articles 31 and 32 of the Vienna Convention on the Law of Treaties,[2] either because it is a treaty binding upon the host State and the State of which the investor is a national, or else because it is considered a manifestation of customary law as the International Court of Justice (ICJ) has repeatedly recognized.[3] However, reference to these articles does not necessarily illuminate the approach to interpretation chosen by the tribunal. Articles 31 and 32 of the Vienna Convention are themselves a compromise among different approaches:

[1] '[T]here is nothing inevitable to the selection of any particular approach to interpretation. There are choices everywhere'. Sunstein, *Legal Reasoning and Political Conflict* 33. 'The use of original meaning, in the interpretation of texts, is a choice – the selection of a particular interpretive strategy – and the choice needs to be defended with reasons . . . any approach to interpretation requires a justification of some kind . . . ' ibid., 170.

[2] Vienna Convention on the Law of Treaties, Vienna, in force 27 January 1980, 1155 UNTS 331.

[3] In this respect it is interesting to note the following comment on the state of customary law on treaties at the time of the Convention preparation by the International Law Commission: 'En bref, la C.D.I. est face à des indices sérieux, mais pas toujours concordants, qui lui permettent d'élaborer une codification de l'interprétation sans la certitude que la base est fermement coutumière. L'affirmation de la sentence du Lac Lanoux en 1957 résume ces incertitudes: "Le droit international ne consacre aucun système absolu d'interprétation". La C.D.I. va ainsi donner l'impression de codifier des principes coutumiers d'interprétation alors que le socle est fragile. C'est plus la Convention elle-même qui va rendre ces principes coutumiers et les projecter dans l'avenir comme s'ils l'avaient toujours été': J.M. Sorel, 'Interprétation des traités' in O. Corten and P. Klein (eds.), *Les conventions de Vienne sur le droit des traités: commentaire article par article*, vol. II (Brussels: Bruylant, 2006), Part 3, Section 3, para. 15.

compromise entre les tenants de l'interprétation textuelle, de l'interprétation subjective basé sur la volonté des parties, et de l'interprétation téléologique qui tente d'extirper du texte tout ce que ce dernier peut induire au-delà des mots utilisés. Nous sommes face à un article qui mêle les moyens permettant l'interprétation (le texte, le contexte et les circonstances) et les manières d'envisager ces moyens, autrement dit les méthodes. L'objectif est de rechercher une interprétation à la fois évidente (sens ordinaire des termes), logique (acte clair) et efficace (effet utile).[4]

How the different approaches embedded in these articles relate to each other is a matter of disagreement. For some, the concepts of original meaning, context and purpose do not comprise a list to be strictly applied but rather express a hierarchical preference.[5] For others, these approaches are bolted together into a unitary list to be followed, even though 'the contradictory implications of such a listing' are not resolved.[6] References to the Convention provide legitimacy to the interpretation itself,[7] but tend

[4] Ibid., para. 9. Furthermore, 'priorité au texte mais intention des parties sous-jacente dans de nombreux passages, et une interprétation finaliste qui peut être réintégrée aux processus d'ensemble. Il faut donc constater que la Convention juxtapose des principes parfois contradictories qui peuvent aboutir – avec les mêmes instruments – à des conclusions fort éloignées. Interprétation et sécurité juridique semblent parfois antinomiques, tant es grande la liberté laissée à l'interprète. Ces aspects expliquent probablement que la base et les méthodes codifiés n'aient jamais réellement été remises en cause', ibid., para. 58.

[5] In considering Article 31, para. 1 of the Vienna Convention, Aust opines that object and purpose is an elusive concept: 'Fortunately, the role it plays in interpreting treaties is less than the search for the ordinary meaning of the words in their context. In practice, having regard to the object and purpose is more for the purpose of confirming an interpretation. If an interpretation is incompatible with the object and purpose, it may well be wrong. Thus, although paragraph 1 contains both the textual (or literal) and the effectiveness (or teleological) approaches, it gives precedence to the textual': A. Aust, *Modern Treaty Law and Practice* (2nd edn, Cambridge University Press, 2007), 235.

[6] The sequence in Article 31, para. 1 of the Vienna Convention is not one of precedence, but at most of logical progression: 'The debates within the International Law Commission also show very little consensus about how these different topical considerations could be systematized through establishing clear rules of priority among the principles of interpretation . . . Listing the "good faith" requirement . . . together with the "ordinary meaning", the "context", and the "purposes" shows merely that several topoi have been bolted together without resolving the contradictory implications of such a listing': F.V. Kratochwil, *Rules, Norms and Decisions: On the Conditions of Practical and Legal Reasoning in International Relations and Domestic Affairs* (Cambridge University Press,1989), 235.

[7] 'The *Ad hoc* Committee notes on this point first that the Tribunal did not identify or describe in its Award the rules of interpretation it proposed to apply. The applicable "law" can be considered to have been the rules codified in Article 31 and subsequent Articles of the Vienna Convention. The question therefore arises whether the Tribunal applied these rules or whether there was a failure in this regard amounting to an excess of powers. Indeed, there are some elements regarding the interpretation of Article 2 of the BIT which the *Ad hoc* Committee would have expected to find in an award applying

to remain at the general level and, once the reference has been made, the result may not match the stated method.[8] For instance, in *Berschader* v. *Russia*, the Tribunal professed to be guided by Article 31 of the Vienna Convention, but the majority used as the starting point of its analysis the 'assessment of the intention of the contracting parties upon the conclusion of the original treaty'.[9] The Tribunal turned to the text of the treaty only after concluding that no case law was directly on point in respect of the definition of investment.[10] The dissenting arbitrator pointed out that the treaty terms themselves are the best evidence of ascertaining such intent.[11] The *Inceysa* Tribunal considered the *travaux préparatoires* as a method to find the parties' intention without first analysing the text[12] as prescribed by Article 31 and ignored that recourse to *travaux préparatoires* is limited under Article 32 'to confirm the meaning resulting from the application of Article 31, or to determine the meaning when the interpretation according to Article 31: (a) leaves the meaning ambiguous or obscure; or (b) leads to a result which is manifestly absurd or unreasonable'.[13]

A tribunal has described interpretation under Article 31 of the Vienna Convention as 'a process of progressive encirclement where the interpreter starts with (1) the ordinary meaning of terms of the treaty, (2) in their context and (3) in light of the treaty's object and purpose, and by cycling through this three step inquiry iteratively closes in upon the proper interpretation'.[14] As observed by the same tribunal, the Vienna Convention does not give

international rules of treaty interpretation based on the Vienna Convention': *Industria Nacional de Alimentos, SA and Indalsa Perú, SA (formerly Empresas Lucchetti, SA and Lucchetti Perú, SA)* v. *Republic of Perú*, ICSID Case No. ARB/03/4 (Peru/Chile BIT). Decision on Annulment, 5 September 2007, paras. 113–14 available at: http://ita.law.uvic.ca/documents/LucchettiAnnulment.pdf.

[8] 'La référence à la Convention de 1969 légitime l'interprétation même si une fois la reference énoncé, le résultat ne correspond guère à la méthode énoncée': Corten and Klein, *Les conventions de Vienne*, para. 59.

[9] *Berschader* v. *The Russian Federation*, SCC Case No. 080/2004, Award, 21 April 2006, para. 206, available at: http://ita.law.uvic.ca/documents/BerschaderFinalAward.pdf.

[10] Ibid., para. 136. [11] Ibid., Separate Opinion, para. 4.

[12] *Inceysa Vallisoletana, S.L.* v. *Republic of El Salvador*, ICSID Case No. ARB/03/26, Award, 2 August 2006, para. 192 ff, available at: http://ita.law.uvic.ca/documents/Inceysa_Vallisoletana_en_001.pdf.

[13] See further section 6. below, 'The weight of the non-disputing State party' and M.H. Arsanjani and W. Michael Reisman, 'Interpreting Treaties for the Benefit of Third Parties: The "Salvors Doctrine" and the Use of Legislative History in Investment Treaties' *AJIL* 104 (2010) 597.

[14] *Aguas del Tunari SA* v. *Republic of Bolivia*, ICSID Case No. ARB/02/3, Decision on Respondent's Objections to Jurisdiction, 21 October 2005, para. 91, available at: http://ita.law.uvic.ca/documents/AguasdelTunari-jurisdiction-eng_000.pdf.

preference to any of the three steps, but it would seem that the exercise is incomplete if all three are not followed. This process places before the interpreter the elements that he has to take into consideration. Only then, in the words of Sir Ian Sinclair, 'he will be in a position to assess their relative value and weight in the light of the rules laid down in the Convention'.[15]

The interpretative principles set forth in the Vienna Convention do not include a specific method for determining the relative value and weight of the three elements in reaching a decision. The Convention does not guide adjudicators when to choose a broad or narrow interpretation, when to choose between legal form and economic reality, or how to determine when an interpretation is 'balanced'. It merely provides a useful springboard for a tribunal to start the search for meaning.[16] Furthermore, there are aspects of treaty interpretation left out of the Convention:

> l'article 31 laisse dans l'ombre quelques aspects qui n'ont pu être résolus, ou que l'on n'a pas souhaité résoudre. L'effet utile n'est pas mentionné car il est considéré comme implicite dans la bonne foi, et implicite dans la lumière de l'objet et du but du traité, ce qui peut laisser la place à une interprétation à tendance téléologique. Le droit intertemporel est également évincé pour éviter une presumption en faveur de la régle en vigueur à l'époque de la conclusion du traité, ou à l'époque de son interprétation. L'adage selon lequel 'les limitations à la souveraineté ne se présument pas' est également passé sous silence, sa connotation étant sans doute trop forte en dépit d'une base jurisprudentielle.[17]

The tensions built into Article 31 of the Vienna Convention frequently surface in the context of treaty interpretations by arbitral tribunals. In general, tribunals subscribe to the ideal of producing a balanced interpretation, but the recurring issue is how to achieve such an interpretation. Treaties may provide for multiple purposes which need to be taken into account when seeking a balanced interpretation and tribunals may face dilemmas when attempting to give effect to certain provisions at the risk of allowing detriment to others. Tribunals may appeal to common sense or consider

[15] I. Sinclair, *The Vienna Convention on the Law of Treaties* (2nd edn, Manchester University Press, 1984), 73.

[16] Raz: 'All too often interpretation is just a matter of reasoning to a reasonable view on the basis of a variety of considerations, some reinforcing each other, some clashing. There is no way of reducing such reasoning to the application of rules, or other norms, nor is there any way of eliminating the need and desirability of interpretations that consists in and results from such reasoning'. Quoted by A. Barak, *Purposive Interpretation of Law* (Princeton University Press, 2005), 210.

[17] Sorel, 'Interpretation destraités', para. 27.

certain terms clear, and such appeals or determinations point to an underlying choice made by each tribunal whether to provide explicit reasoning or whether to offer merely a conclusion. The interpretation of the silence of the treaty on a particular contested matter will require a tribunal to choose between certain presumptions. To what extent should the absence of the non-disputing State party be taken into account in the interpretation of the treaty concerned? We will review these topics in the following sections.

1. Clarity and common sense

Clarity of meaning and common sense are considered together because they have a characteristic in common: the tribunal appealing to either attribute assumes that certain understandings are commonly shared and, hence, do not need further justification.

The subjectivity of a determination that a text is clear becomes evident when awards interpreting similar provisions are considered to be clear by one tribunal and not by another. The determination that a text is clear is a conclusion rather than a reason. It precludes a tribunal from giving weight to other interpretative elements such as context or purpose. The *Berschader* Tribunal considered it unnecessary to take into account the statement of the Belgian Ministers to Parliament when they presented the investment treaty between Belgium–Luxembourg and Russia because the contested language was 'quite clear' and 'could not possibly' lend itself to the interpretation given by the two Ministers.[18] On the other hand, the *Renta* Tribunal disputed the clarity of a similar clause and gave 'weight to the Belgian Foreign Ministers' unequivocal explanation . . . of their understanding of an identical text – not so much as an expression of intent as the reflection of a proper reading to the effect that an international tribunal could decide whether there was a duty to compensate for an expropriatory measure'.[19]

As in the case of 'clarity', tribunals that appeal to common sense[20] or qualify the result of an interpretation as absurd generally assume that they are applying certain shared values and have no need to specify them. When

[18] *Berschader*, para. 158. [19] *Renta*, para. 59.

[20] '"Common sense" has a dual role to play, as implying the sort of rough contemporary consensus on social values to which judges conceive of themselves as giving effect, and as covering the test for consistency of two possible objectives, to decide what makes pursuing one "self-defeating" in the context of pursuit of the other'. N. MacCormick, *Legal Reasoning and Legal Theory* (Oxford: Clarendon Press, 1978), 149.

the *Methanex* Tribunal determined what the words 'relating to' investors and investments meant in the phrase 'measures adopted or maintained by a Party relating to' in Article 1101(1) of NAFTA, it rejected the claimant's contention that the government measure had *only to affect* the investor because it would:

produce a surprising, if not an absurd result. The possible consequences of human conduct are infinite, especially when comprising acts of governmental agencies; but common sense does not require that line to run unbroken towards an endless horizon. In a traditional legal context, somewhere the line is broken; and whether as a matter of logic, social policy or other value judgment, a limit is necessarily imposed restricting the consequences for which that conduct is to be held accountable.[21]

The Tribunal recognized the role of value judgments in deciding whether 'the line is broken' and it conceded that the exact dividing line was not easy to define: 'just as it is not easy in twilight to see the divide between night and day. Nonetheless, whilst the exact line may remain undrawn, it should still be possible to determine on which side of the divide a particular claim must lie'.[22] The *Methanex* Tribunal did not undertake the task of drawing the line and appealed to common sense to decide that the position advanced by the claimant would produce a surprising or absurd result. The Tribunal presupposed that there was a consensus on the values underlying the decision and, in consequence, did not consider it necessary to give further reasons.[23] From this perspective, appeal to common sense may be questionable in an area of the law still unsettled and where consensus remains elusive.

[21] *Methanex Corporation* v. *United States of America*, Partial Award on Jurisdiction and Admissibility, 7 August 2002, 7 ICSID Reports 239, para. 138.

[22] Ibid., para. 139.

[23] '"Common sense" and similar arguments are best understood as appeals to widely accepted substantive reasons and are, therefore, policy arguments . . . even if they are rather abbreviated policy discussions.' J. Bell, *Policy Arguments in Judicial Decisions* (Oxford: Clarendon Press, 1983), 36. 'The criticism which is sometimes leveled at judges for ignoring the policy questions involved in their decisions might properly be understood as criticism of the judges for being too ready to assume that there is no fundamental disagreement about the values to be applied, so that they are content to invoke "common sense" and other expressions which explain little about the reasons justifying their decision.' Ibid. 'Common sense is what "everyone knows" without having to think hard about a subject. So it is elliptical, like intuition. And it is culturally specific. But within a culture it is a valid though a flawed source of knowledge. It operates in judicial decision making as a set of policy judgments that everyone agrees on and so are not thought political at all': R. Posner, *How Judges Think* (Cambridge, Mass.: Harvard University Press, 2008), 116–17.

2. Balance between purposes

The preamble to investment treaties normally reflects the parties' agreement to promote and protect investments made by individuals and companies, nationals of one party, in the territory of the other. For instance, in the UK investment treaties, the parties express the desire 'to create favorable conditions for greater investment by investors of one State in the territory of the other' and recognize that 'the encouragement and reciprocal protection under international law of such investments will be conducive to the stimulation of individual business initiative and will increase prosperity in both States'. Some, including those of the UK, may even include an additional specific covenant committing each party to 'encourage and create favorable conditions for investors of the other Contracting Party to invest capital in its territory, and, subject to its right to exercise powers conferred by its laws, shall admit such capital'.

Construing the preamble as part of the context and purpose of the treaty, the tribunal in *SGS* v. *Philippines* found it legitimate to resolve uncertainties in favour of the protection of covered investments.[24] It refused to read into the clause the limitation argued by the Philippines that, if the clause had to have an operative effect, it would be circumscribed to obligations under other international law instruments. The Tribunal was of the view that such a limitation could 'readily' have been expressed in the text of the treaty, but the parties had not done so.[25] It also considered the approach adopted by the Tribunal in the *SGS* v. *Pakistan* arbitration, and found that the reliance placed by that Tribunal upon general principles of international law as a means to generate a presumption against the broad interpretation of the umbrella clause was unjustified.[26]

On the other hand, the Tribunal in *Saluka* v. *Czech Republic* sought to balance the two main purposes of the treaty, and considered the effect of excessive protection on the promotion of investments. According to the Tribunal, an interpretation which exaggerates the protection to be accorded to foreign investments may dissuade host States from admitting foreign investors to their territory and by so doing undermine the overall aim of extending and intensifying the parties' mutual economic

[24] *SGS Société Générale de Surveillance SA* v. *Republic of the Philippines*, ICSID Case No. ARB/02/6, Decision on Objections to Jurisdiction, 29 January 2004, 8 ICSID Reports 518, para. 116.

[25] Ibid., para. 118. [26] Ibid., para. 122.

relations.[27] In the same vein, the *Renta* Tribunal concluded that: '[t]he long-term promotion of investment is likely to be better ensured by a well-balanced regime rather than by one which goes so far that it provokes a swing of the pendulum in the other direction'.[28]

There is no doubt that the overall content and intention of investment treaties is to protect investors. However, arbitral tribunals in interpreting their purposes may, out of concern for the consequences that an 'excessive' protection would have on the promotion of investments, balance the text by introducing presumptions guided by the preamble to the BIT or by extraneous considerations to the text, such as certain principles of international law. The 'balanced' interpretation will be reached at different points because of the different elements tribunals place in the scales.

3. Balance between purpose and text

When analysing a jurisdictional clause which states 'or concerning any other matter consequential upon an act of expropriation in accordance with Article 5 of this Agreement', the *RosInvestCo* Tribunal reasoned that:

> In a potential analogy with the issue of Kompetenz-Kompetenz, it may be argued that, in order to exercise its undoubted competence to decide a disputed issue consequential on an expropriation, a tribunal must (implicitly) be endowed with the power to determine whether the issue is 'consequential upon an act of expropriation.[29]

But the Tribunal rejected that possible interpretation because it 'would deprive the wording "*or concerning any other matter consequential upon*" in the above-mentioned qualification of any substantive meaning and turn this jurisdictional clause into an arbitration clause'.[30] This is what the *Renta*

[27] 'It is worth [*sic.*] of note that by opening a wide door to foreign parties to commercial contracts concluded with a State-owned company to switch their contractual disputes from normal jurisdiction of international commercial tribunals or state courts to BIT Tribunals, the majority of this Tribunal has created a potentially dangerous precedent capable of producing negative effects on the further development of foreign capital participation in privatizations of State-owned companies': *Eureko B.V.* v. *Republic of Poland*, Partial Award and Dissenting Opinion, 19 August 2005, para. 11, available at: http://ita.law.uvic.ca/documents/Eureko-PartialAwardandDissentingOpinion.pdf.

[28] *Renta*, para. 55. Referring to the statement in *SGS* v. *Philippines*, the *Renta* Tribunal explained that '[t]o "favor the protection of covered investments" is not equivalent to a presumption that the investor is right', para. 57.

[29] *RosInvestCo*, para. 115. [30] Ibid.

Tribunal did on the basis of 'considerations of purposes' with 'a solid foundation':

> It must be accepted that investment is not promoted by purely formal or illusory standards of protection. It must more specifically be accepted that a fundamental advantage perceived by investors in many if not most BITs is that of the internationalization of the host state's commitments. It follows that it is impermissible to read Article 10 of the BIT as a vanishingly narrow internationalization of either Russia's or Spain's commitment.[31]

In dismissing the 'narrow internationalization' in favour of implicit coverage of an act of expropriation under the contested clause, the Tribunal disregarded in part the actual wording of the clause and gave preference to the objectives over the text.

The same Tribunal, however, did not extend its consideration of treaty purposes to the interpretation of whether a reference to treatment in the BIT was only reference to fair and equitable treatment or to treatment more broadly. After noting the lexical difficulties posed by the article of the BIT in question, it concluded that '[s]omething has to give. The choice is between an explicit stipulation and a revelation by grammatical deconstruction. The Tribunal naturally prefers the former.'[32] The dissenting arbitrator appended a separate opinion where he argued that Articles 31 and 32 of the Vienna Convention precluded the existence of such a choice:

> It is rather like Alexander the Great severing the Gordian Knot, instead of untying it, as the ancient King of Phrygia had prescribed, and as I understand the Vienna Convention requires. The result of interpretation may be 'unambiguous', but it nonetheless must result from a process that includes the very 'grammatical deconstruction' rejected by the majority. Under Article 31 of the Vienna Convention one looks not just to the 'ordinary meaning' of a word or words; words must be viewed 'in light of [the treaty's] object and purpose', and in their 'context', which under Article 31(2) of the Convention includes the entire text of the treaty . . .[33]

Whether the text is ambiguous is a rather subjective matter, as exemplified by *Berschader* and *Renta*. In the latter case, the Tribunal was willing to override the text of Article 10 of the treaty because it was not clear enough in view of the treaty's express purposes, but it stopped at the ordinary meaning in the analysis of the text of Article 5 of the treaty on the basis that the text was explicit notwithstanding certain lexical difficulties.

[31] *Renta*, para. 56. [32] Ibid., para. 117.
[33] *Renta*, Separate Opinion of Charles N. Brower, para. 13.

4. Interpretation of silence: the MFN clause controversy

Tribunals faced with a provision which is silent on whether that provision covers a certain matter diverge in their approach to interpretation depending on whether they consider that, if the parties to a treaty had wanted the matter in question covered, they would have provided for it or, conversely, they would have explicitly excluded it if this had been their intent.[34] We have already seen how the *Methanex* Tribunal dealt with the issue of whether it had the power to authorize *amicus curiae*, given the silence of NAFTA and the UNCITRAL Arbitration Rules on the matter. But it is the issue of whether to incorporate coverage of dispute settlement under an MFN clause which is silent on this point that has attracted most controversy. Tribunals have been divided ever since the first two tribunals which considered the issue took opposing views.

In the first case, *Maffezini* v. *Spain*, the Tribunal considered the text of the clause, which referred to all matters, to precedent and to the policies followed by the treaty parties, including the non-disputing party, and concluded:

> Notwithstanding the fact that the basic treaty containing the clause does not refer expressly to dispute settlement as covered by the most favored nation clause, the Tribunal considers that there are good reasons to conclude that today dispute settlement arrangements are inextricably related to the protection of foreign investors, as they are also related to the protection of rights of traders under treaties

[34] Silence raises the issue of who should bear the risk of ambiguity. Should this risk be borne by the investor or the State? Here there are two conflicting replies to the question: First: 'the main principles underlying the NAFTA (preamble Article 102) as developed in the most recent and authoritative jurisprudence by arbitral tribunals require that, in case of doubt, the risk of ambiguity of a governmental assurance is allocated rather to the government than to a foreign investor, and that the government is held to high standards of transparency and responsibility for the clarity and consistency in its interaction with foreign investors': T. Wälde, Separate Opinion appended to Award in *International Thunderbird Gaming Corporation* v. *United Mexican States*, UNCITRAL, 26 January 2006, para. 3324, available at: http://ita.law.uvic.ca/documents/ThunderbirdSeparateOpinion.pdf. In contrast: '[b]ecause investment treaties use such broad language to define core concepts, the presumption in favor of investment protection systematically favors an expansive approach to jurisdiction or, in the case of the standards of review, to state liability. This elevates the norm of investor protection in the same way that doctrines of human rights prioritize certain individual rights over those of the state, and the result is to exaggerate the importance of investor protection in relation to the other values and concerns that are at stake in governmental decision-making': G. van Harten, *Investment Treaty Arbitration and Public Law* (Oxford University Press, 2007), 139.

of commerce. Consular jurisdiction in the past, like other forms of extraterritorial jurisdiction, were considered essential for the protection of rights of traders and, hence, were regarded not merely as procedural devices but as arrangements designed to better protect the rights of such persons abroad. It follows that such arrangements, even if not strictly a part of the material aspect of the trade and investment policy pursued by treaties of commerce and navigation, were essential for the adequate protection of the rights they sought to guarantee.[35]

The *Plama* Tribunal considered the matter at great length, notwithstanding that it did not rely on the MFN clause to assert jurisdiction. This Tribunal used the UK Model BIT as an example and concluded that 'the intention to incorporate dispute settlement provisions must be clearly and unambiguously expressed'.[36] Even when the expression 'with respect to all matters' appears in the MFN provisions, it does not alleviate the doubt of whether it applies to dispute settlement provisions.[37] Similarly, the Tribunal was not convinced that the lack of reference to dispute settlement in the exceptions to MFN treatment meant that all other non-excepted matters would fall within the purview of the clause. Since the exception referred to privileges, the Tribunal reasoned that it may be understood to relate to substantive protection and, therefore, it could be argued with equal force that the MFN clause related to 'substantive protection to the exclusion of the procedural provisions relating to dispute settlement'.[38]

The arguments for and against coverage of dispute settlement as part of MFN treatment have repeated themselves along the lines of *Maffezini* or *Plama* in numerous cases. The *Gas Natural* v. *Argentina* Tribunal considered that, as a matter of principle, MFN provisions in BITs should be understood to be applicable to dispute settlement provisions unless it appears clearly that the parties intended otherwise.[39] The *Berschader* Tribunal applied the converse 'principle':

[35] *Maffezini* v. *Kingdom of* Spain, ICSID Case No. ARB/97/7, Decision on Objections to Jurisdiction, 25 January 2000, 5 ICSID Reports 396, para. 54.

[36] *Plama* v. *Bulgaria*, para. 204.

[37] Ibid., para. 205. The decision says that this point is made in the Decision on Jurisdiction in the case of *Siemens* v. *Argentina*. The reference is mistaken. In that decision the Tribunal deals with the fact that there is no such reference to 'with respect to all matters' in the Germany–Argentina BIT. The *Berschader* Tribunal repeats the mistake by relying on the reference in the *Plama* decision. See *Siemens A.G.* v. *Argentina*, ICSID Case No. ARB/02/8, Decision on Jurisdiction, 3 August 2004, 12 ICSID Reports 174, para. 103.

[38] Ibid., para. 191.

[39] *Gas Natural S.D.G., S.A.* v. *Argentine Republic*, ICSID Case No. ARB/03/10, Decision on Preliminary Questions on Jurisdiction, 17 June 2005, 14 ICSID Reports 284, para. 49.

> the present Tribunal will apply the principle that an MFN provision in a BIT will only incorporate by reference an arbitration clause from another BIT where the terms of the original BIT clearly and unambiguously so provide or where it can otherwise be clearly inferred that this was the intention of the contracting parties... [T]his Tribunal does not derive the requirement for clarity and lack of ambiguity involved in this test from any general principle to the effect that arbitration clauses should be interpreted more restrictively than other agreements. Nevertheless, this test is warranted, in the view of the Tribunal, by the particular problems discussed above which are posed by the construction of the scope of MFN provisions in BITs.[40]

However, this same Tribunal used the opposite reasoning when dealing with the specific exceptions to the MFN clause, which did not exclude jurisdictional matters. In favouring the overall limitation of the clause, the Tribunal did not apply a 'strict' interpretation.

Considering the exception to the MFN clause, the *RosInvest Co* Tribunal had this to say:

> it needs no further explanation that, just as taxation is a highly important matter for an investor, so is the submission to arbitration which 'protects' the investor, should a dispute arise with the Host State, from having to depend on the national courts of the same Host State. In view of the careful drafting of Article 8 and the limiting language therein, it can certainly not be presumed that the Parties 'forgot' arbitration when drafting and agreeing on Article 7. Had the Parties intended that the MFN-clauses should also not apply to arbitration, it would indeed have been easy to add a subsection (c) to that effect in Article 7. The fact that this was not done, in the view of the Tribunal, is further confirmation that the MFN-clauses in Article 3 are also applicable to submissions to arbitration in other Treaties.[41]

Similarly, the *Renta* Tribunal observed that MFN clauses by their very nature suppose an extension of commitments: '[d]rafters wishing to do so would have little difficulty in defining restrictions that would go further than the general *ejusdem generis* constraint... Absent such stipulations it is the task of international tribunals to determine whether arbitration clauses in comparator treaties in fact comport more favored treatment.'[42]

The arguments just surveyed show both the limits of logic in the interpretation of a clause which does not specifically cover the situation at hand and the lack of common values adhered to by tribunals in deciding the matter. They reflect, notwithstanding the statement to the contrary in *Berschader*,

[40] *Berschader*, paras. 181–2. [41] *RosInvestCo*, para. 135. [42] *Renta*, 92.

the controversy on whether consent clauses to arbitration need to be interpreted narrowly, or interpreted for what they say. The issue was not buried by the Vienna Convention, because that instrument simply does not cover it.[43] The minimum limitation of State sovereignty is the implicit starting point which guides the reasoning process and favours a presumption in favour of limiting investment protection, which even the ordinary meaning of a phrase such as 'all matters of concern to this treaty' is not sufficient to override.

5. Interpretation of umbrella clauses

There are many versions of umbrella clauses, and I will be referring to the clauses in the style used in the UK BITs: 'Each Contracting Party shall observe any obligation it may have entered into with regards to investments of investors of the other Contracting Party.' Second, I understand 'obligation entered into' as a contractual obligation and not as referring to legislative provisions which may have given rise to certain expectations. Third, I understand 'entered into' as referring to a specific contract between the foreign investor and the State. Fourth, it should be a contract that qualifies as an investment.

Within the field delimited thus, the approaches of the tribunals have varied according to the weight they have given to, first, the separation of the domestic and international legal orders and, second, the principle of effectiveness in interpreting a text. Crawford has identified four schools of thought in the case law.[44] At one extreme, there is the application of the clause by internationalizing contract claims in full without even discussing the issue of the forum chosen in the contract. *Fedax* and *Eureko* are the salient examples of this school.[45] At the other end, the concern for the principle that breaches of contracts are not breaches of international law

[43] 'the Vienna Convention represents a move away from the canons of interpretation previously common in treaty interpretation and which erroneously persist in various international decisions today. For example, the Vienna Convention does not mention the canon that treaties are to be construed narrowly, a canon that presumes States can not have intended to restrict their range of action': *Aguas del Tunari* v. *Bolivia*, para. 91. Compare with comment of J.M. Sorel at footnote 64.

[44] J. Crawford, 'Treaty and Contract in Investment Arbitration' *Arbitration International* 24 (2008) 351, 367.

[45] *Fedax N.V.* v. *Venezuela*, ICSID Case No. ARB/96/3, Decision on Jurisdiction, 11 June 1997, 5 ICSID Reports 186; Award, 9 March 1998, 5 ICSID Reports 200, para. 29; *Eureko B.V* v. *Republic of Poland*, *ad hoc* Arbitration, Partial Award, 19 August 2005, 12 ICSID Reports 331, paras. 244–60.

drives tribunals to interpret the clause so restrictively that it divests it of any practical meaning. This is the case in *SGS* v. *Pakistan*.[46] Somewhere in between, the umbrella clause is reduced to cover only breaches resulting from the State acting as a sovereign. In the fourth approach, 'an umbrella clause is operative and may form the basis for a substantive treaty claim, but it does not convert a contractual claim into a treaty claim'.[47]

The last is the preferred approach of Crawford, and was adopted by the majority in the *SGS* v. *Philippines* award.[48] He calls this solution the 'integrationist view', because it maintains the distinction between treaty and contract and fulfils the purpose of the umbrella clause 'to allow enforcement without internationalization and without transforming the character and content of the underlying obligation'.[49]

To Crawford's four approaches I would add a fifth category: this fifth type of approach involves taking into account the international obligation of the disputing State to the other State party of the BIT. But before addressing this new fifth category, I will review in some detail the reasoning behind the choices of the arbitral tribunals in the two *SGS* cases, including the dissenting opinion of one of the arbitrators in the *Philippines* case, so that it is easier to understand where the fifth category fits in.

The Tribunal in the *SGS* v. *Pakistan* case expressed the need for clear and convincing evidence that it was the shared intent of the contracting parties to do away with the principle of international law that a breach of contract is not necessarily a breach of international law. The Tribunal was concerned that the claimant's interpretation of the umbrella clause was susceptible of almost infinite expansion.[50] In rejecting the claimant's contention, the Tribunal gave at least three reasons: first, such an interpretation would 'amount to incorporating by reference an unlimited number of State contracts, as well as other municipal law instruments setting out State commitments including unilateral commitments to an investor of the other Contracting Party'.[51] Second, it would make the substantive

[46] *SGS Société Générale de Surveillance S.A.* v. *Islamic Republic of Pakistan*, ICSID Case No. ARB/01/13, Decision on Objections to Jurisdiction, 6 August 2003, 8 ICSID Reports 406, paras. 163–74.

[47] Crawford, 'Treaty and Contract in Investment Arbitration', 368.

[48] *SGS Société Générale de Surveillance S.A.* v. *Republic of the Philippines*, ICSID Case No. ARB/02/6, Decision on Objections to Jurisdiction, 29 January 2004, 8 ICSID Reports 515.

[49] Crawford, 'Treaty and Contract in Investment Arbitration', at 370.

[50] *SGS* v. *Pakistan*, para. 166.

[51] Ibid., para. 168.

protections of the treaty superfluous. Third, it would nullify negotiated disputed settlement clauses and 'the investor could always defeat the State's invocation of the contractually specified forum, and render any mutually agreed procedure of dispute settlement a dead-letter, at the investor's choice. The investor would remain free to go to arbitration either under the contract or under the BIT. But the State party to the contract would be effectively precluded from proceeding to the arbitral forum specified in the contract unless the investor was minded to agree'.[52]

In dismissing the argument based on the *Pakistan* Tribunal's decision, the *SGS* v. *Philippines* Tribunal noted that the umbrella clause was 'far from elevating to the international level all "the municipal legislative or administrative or other unilateral measures of a Contracting Party"'.[53] It was 'limited to "obligations . . . assumed with regard to specific investments . . . " [T]he host State must have assumed a legal obligation, and it must have been assumed vis-à-vis the specific investment – not as a matter of the application of some legal obligation of a general character.'[54] The *Philippines* Tribunal also found unjustified the reliance of the *Pakistan* Tribunal on general principles of international law to generate a presumption against the broad interpretation of the umbrella clause.[55]

On the other hand, the *Philippines* Tribunal held that an umbrella clause could not override a contract forum clause. In the words of the Tribunal, '[t]he question is whether a party should be allowed to rely on a contract as the basis of its claim when the contract itself refers that claim exclusively to another forum'. The Tribunal was of the view that this is 'more naturally considered as a matter of admissibility than jurisdiction'.[56] Thus, the claimant should comply with the contract at the basis of its claim in the first place. The Tribunal found that it would have jurisdiction to consider claims under the umbrella clause but that, in the circumstances of the case, the claim was premature, and so it stayed the proceedings and 'must await the determination of the amount payable in accordance with the contractually-agreed process'.[57]

The dissenting arbitrator, Crivellaro, found the argument developed by the majority to be inconsistent. On one hand, the Tribunal declared that it had jurisdiction over SGS's purely contractual claims even though, on the other, it was apparently restricting its jurisdiction merely to BIT claims by only allowing SGS to return its claims to the Tribunal on the basis of

[52] Ibid. [53] *SGS* v. *Philippines*, para. 121. [54] Ibid. [55] Ibid., para. 122.
[56] Ibid., para. 154. [57] Ibid., 163.

a denial of justice.[58] In Crivellaro's opinion, when a provision intended to confer an advantage on a certain party has two possible meanings, the correct answer is given by the principle of law which produces the meaning more favourable to the beneficiary. What is at issue is 'whether an investor's commitment – acceptance of local jurisdiction – remains irrevocable also after that [*sic.*], thanks to a subsequent treaty, the investor has become the beneficiary of a more favorable treatment, including the privilege to chose other forums'.[59]

It is time to return to the fifth alternative. None of the previous approaches has considered whether a State party to an investment treaty breaches the commitments made to the other State party when it insists that an investor sign a forum clause which excludes the arbitration venue in that treaty. Would it not be appropriate for a tribunal established under that investment treaty to uphold the promises of the disputing State party to the other State party in priority to the commitments made by the investor? As for existing contracts, would not the State parties to a treaty have offered an alternative forum by way of that very treaty?[60] Since I posed these questions at the time I delivered these lectures, an arbitral tribunal has dismissed an objection to jurisdiction based on the contractual choice of forum along the lines sketched above:

> in a more general manner, the Arbitral Tribunal observes that Argentina's interpretation, if generally applied, would make it possible for governments to avoid their treaty obligations as regards important matters such as expropriation by the simple expedient of inserting clauses in their contracts that vitiated the right to international arbitration, thereby effectively rendering the arbitration provisions of a bilateral investment treaty a nullity. This would seem inconsistent with a state's basic obligation under international law to implement its treaty obligations in good faith.[61]

58 *SGS* v. *Philippines*, ICSID Case No. ARB/02/6, Declaration of A. Crivellaro, 29 January 2004, 8 ICSID Reports 568, para. 12.

59 Ibid., para. 10.

60 'A treaty cause of action is not the same as a contractual cause of action; it requires a clear showing of conduct which is in the circumstances contrary to the relevant treaty standard. The availability of local courts ready and able to resolve specific issues independently may be a relevant circumstance in determining whether there has been a breach of international law . . . But it is not dispositive, and it does not preclude an international tribunal from considering the merits of the dispute': *Compañía de Aguas del Aconquija S.A. and Comagnie Générale des Eaux/ Vivendi Universal* v. *Argentine Republic*, ICSID Case No. ARB/97/3, Decision on Annulment, 3 July 2002, 6 ICSID Reports 340, para. 113.

61 *TSA Spectrum de Argentina S.A.* v. *Argentine Republic*, ICSID Case No. ARB/05/5, Award, 19 December 2008, para. 63, available at: http://ita.law.uvic.ca/documents/TSAAwardEng.pdf.

Preference for the national order over the international order or vice versa has the effect of diminishing the *effet utile* of a forum clause at the expense of the other, or else undermining the exclusivity of the contract forum clause at the expense of the ICSID jurisdiction contracted by the two States. We can look at the two options just as Buridan's ass looked at two equal bales of hay and, not knowing which one to choose, died of hunger. Tribunals need to decide and they have done it on the basis of the consequences flowing from one choice or another but ignoring, except for *TSA*, whether the respondent State fulfilled its obligation to the other treaty party to offer arbitration to investors. The argument that by pursuing arbitration the claimant breaches its contractual forum clause has its counterpart in the argument that the State breaches its commitment to the other State party when it requires a party to a contract to renounce such venue or object on that basis to the jurisdiction of the Tribunal. For an international arbitration tribunal which is supposed to apply the treaty, it would seem that the rational choice should be to give full effect to the arbitration option agreed between the States.

This discussion shows the difficulty in maintaining the distinction between the international and national legal orders, and in fitting the realities of mixed investment arbitration within traditional moulds. In a commentary written in 1996, Jennings considered that 'the strictly dualistic view of the relationship between international and municipal law is becoming less serviceable and the old well-defined boundaries between public international law and private law are no longer boundaries but grey areas'.[62] The issues just discussed are a telling example.

6. The weight of the non-disputing State party

The nature of investment treaty arbitration is such that by definition one of the State parties to the treaty will not be party to the dispute, and so will not participate in the proceedings. NAFTA, the Central American Free Trade Agreement (CAFTA) or recent US Free Trade Agreements provide institutional mechanisms for non-disputing State party participation and for binding interpretation of the treaty concerned,

[62] R.Y. Jennings, 'The Judiciary, International and National, and the Development of International Law' *ICLQ* 45 (1996) 4. For a detailed analysis of problems posed by the mixed nature of this type of arbitration, see Z. Douglas, 'The Hybrid Foundations of Investment Treaty Arbitration' *BYIL* 74 (2004) 151.

but this is the exception rather than the rule in investment treaty arbitration.[63]

Arbitral tribunal requests for assistance of the non-disputing State are rare. The *Aguas del Tunari* Tribunal was prompted to request assistance from the Netherlands government following the assertion made by the respondent, Bolivia, that both parties to the treaty were on record as declaring that the BIT did not apply to the case. The alleged position of the Dutch government was based on replies of ministers to questions raised by members of the Dutch Parliament. The Dutch response did not assist the Tribunal because, according to the arbitral Tribunal, the government did not provide an 'interpretative position of general application'.[64] Similarly, an interpretation by the parties to the treaty in the *Gruslin* case before initiation of the arbitral proceedings was considered 'a source of confusion rather than clarity' by the Tribunal.[65]

The problem of the lack of participation of one of the State parties is highlighted by the Swiss reaction to the *SGS* v. *Pakistan* case. The Tribunal declined jurisdiction and, after the award was issued, the Swiss government sent a letter to the Deputy Secretary-General of ICSID expressing its alarm 'about the very narrow interpretation given to the meaning of [the umbrella clause] by the Tribunal, which not only runs counter to the intention of Switzerland when concluding the Treaty but is quite evidently neither supported by the meaning of similar articles in BITs by other countries nor by academic comments on such provisions'.[66] Switzerland also wondered why the arbitral tribunal had not sought its opinion on the meaning of the controversial clause.

Thus a tribunal will normally have access only to the interpretation of the disputing State party and to the private party's understanding of the treaty. Both parties to the dispute may provide documentation to support their respective interpretations, such as transmittal reports prepared on the occasion of the submission of the treaty for approval to Parliament or the

63 The investment treaty between Belgium and Burundi is unusual in that it requires negotiations between the two States before the investor may initiate arbitration proceedings.

64 *Aguas del Tunari*, para. 258. An interpretation by the Netherlands and the Czech Republic of certain points which arose in the Partial Award in the *CME* case was submitted to the *CME* Tribunal before the final award. It was taken into account by the Tribunal: *CME Czech Republic BV (The Netherlands)* v. *Czech Republic*, UNCITRAL, Final Award, 14 March 2003, 9 ICSID Reports 264.

65 *Philippe Gruslin* v. *Malaysia*, Award, 27 November 2000, ICSID Case No. ARB/99/3, para. 23.16.

66 *Eureko*, para. 254.

executive.[67] Generally the Tribunal will not have the direct views of the State party which most likely drafted the model document on which the treaty at issue is based. How should this absence affect the interpretation approach of the Tribunal? We may find guidance in a recent instance of annulment under the ICSID Convention. A dissenting member of the *Lucchetti* Annulment Committee opined that this 'circumstance surely imposes a particular duty of caution on the Tribunal' when evaluating the arguments of the disputing treaty party, particularly when the Tribunal is aware of a disagreement between the State parties. He criticized the award for accepting at 'its face value the assertions of the Respondent as to its meaning without some sufficient objective evidence to back them up'.[68]

In *RosInvestCo* the Tribunal was aware of the conflicting starting positions of the treaty parties in respect of the power of the Tribunal to determine whether an expropriation had occurred. One of the arbitrators added a declaration in the middle of the text of the award – an unusual technique – stating that the article in question was:

> on its very face, a difficult compromise between opening positions of the two Contracting States . . . In a circumstance of that kind – which one encounters from time to time in treaty practice – it will seldom if ever be justified for the interpreter to arrive at a conclusion that corresponds to all intents and purposes with the position of either the one Contracting State or that of the other.[69]

In the case of *Renta*, the Tribunal had no official comment from Spain on the interpretation of the disputed provision of the investment treaty with Russia. Because that provision was 'virtually identical' to a similar provision in the investment treaty between Spain and Belgium/Luxembourg, the *Renta* Tribunal considered Belgium's understanding of the provision as reflected in the explanation of the Ministers of Foreign Affairs and Foreign Trade to their Parliament in an official *Exposé des motifs* that the treaty they were recommending for ratification allowed arbitration 'in all areas covered by Article 5 [the disputed provision]' of the treaty. The Tribunal concluded that '[i]t would be unimaginable in this light that the Ministers

[67] The *Generation Ukraine* Tribunal gave considerable weight to the commentary in the US Letter of Submittal, even when Ukraine said that it did not necessarily reflect its official view. The Tribunal noted that Ukraine did not tender any documents emanating from official Ukrainian sources: *Generation Ukraine, Inc.* v. *Ukraine*, ICSID Case No. ARB/00/9, Award, 16 September 2003, 10 ICSID Reports 240, paras. 15.4–15.6.

[68] *Lucchetti* v. *Peru*, Decision on Annulment, Dissenting Opinion of Sir Franklin Berman, para. 9.

[69] *RosInvestCo*, 76.

had understood that the respondent State could avoid Article 10 by claiming that it did not allow arbitrators to determine whether there had been a compensable event at all'.[70]

Except in the cases of binding interpretations pointed out earlier, there is no guarantee that the State parties to a treaty would agree on a disputed point in an ongoing arbitration. The uncertainty at the root of a disputed interpretation may have been a matter of disagreement between the parties to the treaty when it was negotiated. This may have been the issue between Switzerland and Pakistan when they bargained over the text of the umbrella clause, which is a watered-down version of the equivalent clause in the agreement between Switzerland and the Philippines.

It has already been noted that tribunals need not necessarily apply the provisions of Article 31, of the Vienna Convention in the order set forth in that article and that they have recourse to the preparatory work of a treaty before applying Article 31, or in circumstances not prescribed in Article 32. The recourse to preparatory work in a situation where one of the parties to the treaty is not party to the arbitration has consequences for the balance between the parties in dispute, since the private party most likely will not have access to the preparatory work. 'When treaties are designed to induce private parties that did not participate in the negotiations to rely upon their terms and to do specific things, fundamental principles of legality argue, even more, for fidelity to a method based on the text and on post-text events that are available to the parties and are expressive of their agreement.'[71] This comment was prompted by the following statement of the *ad hoc* Annulment Committee in *Malaysian Historical Salvors*: 'courts and tribunals interpreting treaties regularly review the *travaux préparatoires* whenever they are brought to their attention; it is mythological to pretend that they do so only when they first conclude that the term requiring interpretation is ambiguous or obscure'.[72] Tribunals do not seem to have been sensitive to the possible consequences of diverting from the prescribed role of preparatory work in the Vienna Convention.

There is merit in tribunals being more active in seeking the views of the non-disputing State when interpreting controversial clauses and, particularly, when the arbitral tribunal is aware that there is a divergence of views

[70] *Renta*, para. 54.
[71] Arsanjani and Reisman, 'Interpreting Treaties for the Benefit of Third Parties', 604.
[72] Application for Annulment, para. 57 available at: www.worldbank.org/icsid/.

between the parties to the treaty in question or before it engages in the analyses of documents which may reflect only one of the parties' views. The Tribunal will have the benefit of knowing the positions of all interested parties and may be able to reach a more balanced and convincing decision.

Part II

The search for limits

Introduction

This part explores the contours of key concepts for the determination of the jurisdiction of arbitral tribunals and of the substantive protection offered by international treaties to foreign investments. Nationality, investment and legitimate expectations are recurrent themes in the awards and decisions of investment treaty arbitrations. How arbitral tribunals approach these key concepts has varied: in some cases they have given precedence to substance over form, for instance in considering consent to arbitration,[1] whereas in others they have respected the corporate form, for instance for purposes of establishing the nationality of the claimant (except where it has been determined that it was used for fraudulent purposes).

The first chapter of this part addresses issues both of form and of substance in two of these key areas: the nationality of corporations and consent to ICSID arbitration. The second chapter explores the approaches followed by arbitral tribunals to delimit the concept of 'investment', dealing more specifically with the approach adopted by some tribunals pursuant to which the characteristics of an investment, normally assessed in the context of the definition of 'investment', have been given jurisdictional weight. The third chapter discusses issues of substantive protection related to risk assumption and the diligence expected of investors, concepts that serve to define their legitimate expectations in the framework of the standards of fair and equitable treatment and full protection and security.

[1] 'Rejecting legal formalism, ICSID tribunals have looked to the economic reality of foreign investment: projects typically involve a group of foreign investors, a local company established as the investment vehicle, and a series of interrelated agreements with the host State and state-owned companies. Despite the complexities of jurisdiction that can arise in these circumstances, ICSID tribunals have interpreted arbitration agreements expansively to cover all aspects of the investment and to afford all parties in interest the protections of the Convention', in W.M. Tupman, 'Case Studies in the Jurisdiction of ICSID' *ICLQ* 35 (1986) 813, 833. This would seem to reflect a general trend in international law already pointed out by Judge Lachs, according to whom the continuation of such trend would allow international law 'to extend its protective wings over the rights of all its subjects. It is therefore significant – and perhaps encouraging – that the decline of formality has run parallel to the substantive expansion and consolidation of international law. It may therefore, perhaps, further contribute to an increase of confidence in law', in M. Lachs, 'Some Reflections on Substance and Form in International Law', in W. Friedmann, L. Henkin and O. Lissitzyn (eds.), *Transnational Law in a Changing Society. Essays in Honor of Philip C. Jessup* (New York: Columbia University Press, 1972), 112.

3

Form or substance: the nationality of corporate claimants

Nationality, like control or investment, is a key term that is undefined in the ICSID Convention. The nationality of claimants is a determinant factor for purposes of finding jurisdiction under the Convention. Yet the test of nationality of corporations is not provided for in the ICSID Convention, and usually the definition of nationality of corporations varies from one investment treaty to another. The most common test of nationality is that of incorporation in a State, but there may be more substantive requirements relating, for instance, to the corporation being controlled by the nationals of a State party, the location of its headquarters, or even the location of its effective management.

The test of nationality in the framework of the ICSID Convention is of special relevance, as it is necessary to establish that the investor is a national of another State party to the Convention. But on some occasions it can also be relevant to determine whether the claimant has the nationality of the host State, when this is necessary to comply with the internal legal requirement that investments be made through local vehicles. In such cases the host State and the foreign investor may agree that, for purposes of ICSID jurisdiction, the locally incorporated entity does not have the nationality of the State of incorporation, since it is subjected to foreign control.

Besides questions of jurisdiction, the nationality of a claimant is relevant for purposes of the *quid pro quo* established in the ICSID Convention: the right of the investor to sue the host State entails the obligation for the national State of the investor to refrain from intervening diplomatically. This bargain may not be relevant in UNCITRAL cases unless the BIT concerned provides for a similar obligation.

Similarly, NAFTA, CAFTA and US investment treaties generally include the right for a State party to deny benefits to a company of another State party and to the investments made by that company, if the company's investors belong to a third State and said company does not have sufficient business activities in the State party where it is incorporated.[1] The Energy Charter Treaty includes a similar provision.[2] All these provisions aim at establishing a substantial link between a potential claimant and the relevant treaties.

Investments are usually part of complex operations structured through chains of companies which may have different nationalities. What does 'control' mean in these complex structures? Does it refer to the immediate controller, the ultimate controller, or to any of the companies in the chain which happen to have the nationality of a State party to the ICSID Convention and a convenient investment treaty? At what level of this structure should the search for the nationality link of a corporation with a State party stop? In the case of ICSID proceedings in particular, would it be permissible for the national State of one of the companies in the chain of control to intervene diplomatically in favour of a company that is part of the chain of control, but not party to the arbitral proceedings? Does it make a difference whether the State that intervenes diplomatically on behalf of the corporation not party to the arbitral proceedings is a Contracting Party to ICSID?

In addressing these issues the arbitrator is faced with a choice between the investor's or the State's perspective on the matter: it can either uphold the certainty of BIT protection for the investor, or the State's certainty as to whom it is contracting with. In making this choice, should the realities of economic life prevail over legal formalities? How determinant is the knowledge of the host State in relation to who the real investor is and its nationality? Should indirect control by nationals of the host country be a concern? Should arbitral tribunals apply an objective or subjective test to determine foreign control under ICSID Article 25(2)(b)?

I will consider these questions and the choices tribunals have made in the context of four situations: (1) direct and indirect control, (2) transfers of shares, (3) indirect control by nationals of the host State, and (4) misrepresentation of who is the controlling corporation.

1 See, e.g., Art. 1113(2) NAFTA, in force 1 January 1994, (1993) 32 ILM 296; Art. 10.12(2) CAFTA, not yet in force, available at: www.sice.oas.org/Trade/CAFTA/CAFTADR_e/CAFTADRin_e.asp#EiF; US Model BIT (2004), Art. 17, available at: http://ustraderep.gov/Trade_Sectors/Investment/Model_BIT/Section_Index.html.

2 Art. 17 ECT, in force 16 April 1998, 2080 UNTS 100.

1. Direct and indirect control

The question of the nationality of corporations has been present in the case law of ICSID since its early days. In the *AMCO* case, Indonesia argued that the claimant, AMCO Asia, was not a US company because it was controlled by a Mr Tan, of Dutch nationality, through Pan-American, a Hong Kong company of which allegedly Mr Tan was the sole shareholder. The Tribunal rejected the argument, holding that to accept it would mean that 'one should not take into account the legal nationality of the foreign juridical person which controls the local one, but the nationality of the juridical or natural persons who control the controlling juridical person itself: in other words, to take care of a control at the second, and possibly third, fourth, or xth degree'.[3] The Tribunal found the nationality of the direct controlling corporation to be conclusive.

The next time the issue came up the Tribunal took the opposite approach. In *SOABI* v. *Senegal*, the Tribunal allowed the claim to proceed, since the claimant company was indirectly controlled by investors of a State party to ICSID. In that case, SOABI, the claimant company, was incorporated in Senegal, the host State, but was controlled by a foreign company (FLEXA) of Panamanian nationality. Although Panama was not a party to ICSID, the Tribunal found that since FLEXA was in turn controlled by a Belgian investor, the nationality requirement was met, as Belgium was a party to the ICSID Convention. The Tribunal held that the Convention does not require immediate control to determine the nationality of claimants. In its view, Article 25(2)(b) was intended to conciliate, on the one hand, the requirement of host States that investments be carried out through local corporations and, on the other, the willingness of those States to give standing to such locally incorporated companies to be parties in international proceedings under the auspices of ICSID.[4] Likewise, investors may, for their own particular reasons, decide to invest their funds through intermediary companies and still keep the same control of the local company as if they had been direct investors.[5]

The president of the *SOABI* Tribunal, Aron Broches – the architect of the ICSID Convention – appended a declaration to the award where

[3] *Amco Asia Corporation, Pan American Development Ltd and PT Amco Indonesia (AMCO)* v. *Republic of Indonesia*, ICSID Case No. ARB/81/1, Jurisdiction, 25 September 1983, 1 ICSID Reports 389, 396.

[4] *Société Ouest Africaine des Bétons Industriels (SOABI)* v. *Senegal*, ICSID Case No. ARB/82/1, Jurisdiction, 1 August 1984, 2 ICSID Reports 175, para. 35.

[5] Ibid., para. 37.

he dismissed the statement by the *AMCO* Tribunal as *obiter dicta* because the United States, the Netherlands and Hong Kong were all Contracting States to the ICSID Convention and the government of Indonesia was aware of the controlling interest of the US company. In his opinion, the question of direct or indirect control was not determinative in the rejection of the objection to jurisdiction.[6] According to Broches, Article 25(2)(b) of the Convention does not say anything about the character, direct or indirect, of the foreign control which can induce a host State and a foreign investor to treat a company formed under local law as a 'national of another Contracting State': 'the parties should be given the widest latitude to agree on the meaning of "nationality", and any stipulation of nationality made in connection with a conciliation or arbitration clause which is based on a reasonable criterion should be accepted'.[7]

Another member of the Tribunal, Judge Mbaye, took issue with the reasoning of the Tribunal in his dissenting opinion, where he wondered how it could be considered reasonable to subject a State, about to contract with a foreign company, to difficult and sometimes impossible investigations to find out the nationality of the interests of the investment in the labyrinths often created by investors to escape taxation.[8]

2. Transfer of shares

Banro Resource, a Canadian mining company, signed an agreement with the Democratic Republic of Congo (DRC). The agreement contained an ICSID arbitration clause in which the Congolese subsidiary, SAKIMA, was considered to be a foreign national for purposes of the ICSID Convention. Canada was not a party to ICSID. After the DRC repealed the decrees which had approved the Mining Convention, Banro Resource transferred its SAKIMA shares to Banro American, a subsidiary company incorporated in the United States, a State party to the ICSID Convention. Banro American and SAKIMA initiated ICSID proceedings against the DRC. The Tribunal recognized that it could opt for two approaches in the case:

[6] Declaration of President Broches, *SOABI*, Award, 25 February 1988, 2 ICSID Reports 333, para. 4.

[7] Ibid., para. 2, quoting A. Broches, 'The Convention on the Settlement of Investment Disputes between States and Nationals of other States' *Recueil des Cours* 136 (1972) 331, 361.

[8] Mbaye said: '[l]'admettre serait à coup sûr tolérer que l'Etat concerné dans bien des cas soit trompé impunément et son consentement surpris', SOABI, 2 ICSID Reports 277, para. 64.

(a) follow a formal approach and consider Banro American and SAKIMA as the claimants in the case, or (b) follow a substance approach and consider that the real claimants in the case were Banro Resource and SAKIMA. According to the Tribunal, however, neither approach would fulfil requirements of both nationality and consent, necessary to find jurisdiction under the ICSID Convention.

On the first, formal approach, the Tribunal could consider the claimant to have the nationality of a State party to the Convention, yet the requirement of consent would not be met. Indeed, when the DRC entered into the Convention with Banro Resource, it could not have consented to ICSID jurisdiction vis-à-vis that company, since the company was not a national of a State party to the Convention. In consequence, the transfer of shares operated by Banro Resource to Banro American could not have included the right to opt for ICSID arbitration, a right that Banro Resource did not have in the first place, given its Canadian nationality. On the second, substantial approach, the Tribunal could 'go beyond procedural appearances and . . . view the actual Claimants in these arbitration proceedings as the parent company of Banro American, namely Banro Resource, with SAKIMA acting in such a case as the Congolese subsidiary of Banro Resource'.[9] But in this case also one of the requirements for jurisdiction would be missing: although it could be considered that consent to ICSID arbitration existed by virtue of the Convention, the nationality requirement would not be met as Banro Resource, a Canadian company, would not have the nationality of a Contracting State.

The Tribunal did not stop there; it went further and considered whether, given 'the jurisprudence of ICSID tribunals concerning relationship between companies of the same group, the Tribunal could have addressed the issue of *ius standi* of Banro American in a flexible manner'. The Tribunal decided not to do so, because the question went beyond the relationships which existed between groups of companies and raised a fundamental issue of public international law related to the de-politicization of disputes, one of the main goals pursued by the ICSID Convention. Since Canada was not a Contracting State, it would have been free to give diplomatic protection to its national, and Congo could have been subject to diplomatic pressure and possibly inter-State international judicial proceedings. In fact, Canada had intervened diplomatically on behalf of its

[9] *Banro American Resources, Inc and Société Aurifère du Kivu et du Maniema SARL* v. *Democratic Republic of the Congo*, ICSID Case No. ARB/98/7, Award, 1 September 2000, (2002) 17 *ICSID Review – FILJ* 382, para. 7 (excerpts).

national and this may have influenced the thinking of the Tribunal on the matter. Although Article 27 of the Convention – which limits diplomatic protection once arbitral proceedings have been commenced – is addressed to Contracting States, the Tribunal held that when read in conjunction with Article 26 ICSID (exclusive jurisdiction), it precluded the investor from using a plurality of channels to pursue its claims against the host State.

According to the *Banro* Tribunal, ICSID tribunals in similar circumstances 'have rarely proven to be formalistic'.[10] This was the case, in particular, 'when the request was made by a member company of a group of companies while the pertinent instrument expressed the consent of another company of this group; and when, following the transfer of shares, the request came from the transferee company while the consent had been given by the company making the transfer'.[11] ICSID tribunals generally ruled on their jurisdiction by reviewing 'the circumstances surrounding the case, and, in particular, the actual relationships among the companies involved' and basing their decisions on a realistic assessment of the situation.[12] However, in view of the international public policy and international law issues raised by the dispute in question, the Tribunal preferred not to address issues of jurisdiction with the same flexibility as other tribunals, and rejected Banro's claim.

In the case of *Aucoven* v. *Venezuela* (not a BIT case), a Mexican holding company, ICA Holding, had transferred its shares in Aucoven, a Venezuelan corporation, to Icatech, a US company. Venezuela, the host State, approved the transfer. The United States was an ICSID Contracting Party and Mexico was not. Before the Tribunal, Venezuela argued that the definition of 'foreign control' based on formal criteria, such as the direct ownership of the shares, did not fulfil the requirements of Article 25(2)(b) of the ICSID Convention when opposed to the economic reality of the situation in which the ultimate control over Aucoven remained in the hands of the Mexican holding company (ICA Holding), even after the transfer of the shares to Icatech. According to Venezuela, this company was just a shelf Company, and Venezuela claimed that it had been misled when the transfer of shares had taken place.

The Tribunal disagreed. It conceded that economic criteria tended to reflect reality better than legal criteria, but, in the instant case, the arguments based on economic grounds were not appropriate, because the

[10] Ibid., para. 10. [11] Ibid. [12] Ibid., para 11.

parties had used the discretion allowed to them by the ICSID Convention, and had selected the formal criterion of shareholding as the relevant one for the determination of the investment's nationality. The Tribunal found this to be a reasonable criterion to determine control over the claimant.[13] Similarly, the Tribunal found that Icatech was not a mere 'shelf' company and that Venezuela had not been misled at the time it consented to the transfer of shares. The *Aucoven* Tribunal based its finding of jurisdiction on the clause of the investment contract which defined foreign control, and considered that such definition was within the parameters fixed in Article 25 of the ICSID Convention.[14] The Tribunal distinguished this case from *Banro*, where the Tribunal had reached a different conclusion on grounds that, in that case, the transfer of shares was not subject to the approval of the government and the parties had not defined contractually the test of foreign control.[15]

Sir Arthur Watts, who thought that the dismissal of the genuine link argument by the ICJ in the *Barcelona Traction* case sat 'uneasily beside its readiness in the *Nottebohm* case to prefer considerations of substance to those of form',[16] was confronted with this issue as chair of the Tribunal in the *Saluka* case. This Tribunal said that it 'ha[d] some sympathy for the argument that a company which has no real connection with a State party to a BIT, and which is in reality a mere shelf company controlled by another company which is not constituted under the laws of that State,

[13] *Autopista Concesionada de Venezuela (Aucoven), CA* v. *Bolivarian Republic of Venezuela*, ICSID Case No. ARB/00/5, Decision on Jurisdiction, 27 September 2001, 6 ICSID Reports 419, paras. 119–21.

[14] Ibid., para. 142. [15] Ibid., para. 143.

[16] 'The Court's strict regard for the traditional rule and its reluctance to accept additional qualifications establishing an effective link sit uneasily beside its readiness in the *Nottebohm* case to prefer considerations of substance to those of form, and to invoke precedents from "related fields"'. And further, 'It is surprising that the Court was so dismissive, in the context, of the relevance of the kind of "genuine link" it had earlier asserted in relation to natural persons. If, at the international level, the concept of "nationality" comprises considerations of effectiveness in the one context, it would seem appropriate for it also to do so in the other. This is especially so given that in this particular case the company's continuing existence was somewhat tenuous, and that the Court acknowledged that in contemporary circumstances companies were essentially a façade for the shareholders who constituted the reality behind them and that in having regard to institutions of municipal law it was motivated by a concern not to "lose touch with reality"': A Watts, 'Nationality of Claims: Some Relevant Concepts', in V. Lowe and M. Fitzmaurice (eds.), *Fifty Years of the International Court. Essays in Honor of Sir Robert Jennings* (Cambridge University Press, 1996), 432, footnotes omitted.

should not be entitled to invoke the provisions of that treaty'.[17] But, this sympathy notwithstanding:

> the predominant factor which must guide the Tribunal's exercise of its functions is the terms in which the parties to the Treaty... have agreed to establish the Tribunal's jurisdiction... The parties had complete freedom of choice in this matter, and they chose to limit 'investors' to those satisfying the definition set out in Article 1 of the Treaty. The Tribunal cannot in effect impose upon the parties a definition of 'investor' other than that which they themselves agreed.
>
> The Tribunal is confirmed in the appropriateness of the view which it has taken by the consideration... that it was always apparent to the Czech authorities that it was Nomura's intention to transfer the IPB shares it was purchasing to another company within the Nomura Group, and that that other company would be a special-purpose vehicle set up for the specific and sole purpose of holding those shares.[18]

3. Indirect control by nationals of the host State

The Tribunal in *Tokios Tokelės* was confronted with a case in which the claimant was indirectly controlled by nationals of the host State. Tokios Tokelės, an investor company in Ukraine, was a company incorporated in Lithuania, but controlled by nationals of Ukraine. Ukraine objected to the jurisdiction of the Tribunal on grounds that the real claimants had

[17] *Saluka Investments BV* v. *Czech Republic*, PCA, Partial Award, 17 March 2006, para. 240, available at: www.pca-cpa.org/showpage.asp?pag_id=1149.

[18] Ibid., para. 241. Other tribunals have adopted similar approaches. See, e.g., the *Loewen* case, heard under NAFTA, where the Tribunal held that: 'TLGI had filed a voluntary petition for relief under Chapter 11 of the United States Bankruptcy Code, and a reorganization plan was approved by the bankruptcy courts of the United States and Canada. Under that plan, TLGI ceased to exist as a business entity. All of its business operations were reorganized as a United States corporation. In apparent recognition of the obvious problem that would be caused by a United States entity pursuing a claim against the United States under NAFTA, TLGI, immediately prior to its going out of business, assigned all of its right, title and interest to the NAFTA claim to a newly created corporation (discreetly called Nafcanco – a play on the words NAFTA and Canada). It would appear that the NAFTA claim is the only asset of Nafcanco, and the pursuit of the claim its only business... Even if TLGI has some kind of ethereal existence, it sought to place any remaining NAFTA marbles in the Nafcanco ring. Claimants insist that Respondent is asking the Tribunal to "pierce" the corporate veil of Nafcanco and point out the legal complications involved in such a piercing. The Tribunal sees no need to enter into that thicket. The question is whether there is any remaining Canadian entity capable of pursuing the NAFTA claim': *The Loewen Group Inc and Raymond L Loewen* v. *USA*, ICSID Case No. ARB(AF)/98/3, Award, 26 June 2003, 7 ICSID Reports 442, paras. 220, 237.

Ukrainian nationality and no real business in Lithuania or its *siège social*. The majority of the Tribunal rejected the objection, since the investment treaty required only that the claimant be established in Lithuania in accordance with its laws. There was no question of piercing the corporate veil because there was no abuse of legal personality, and the claimant had been established in Lithuania years prior to the signing of the investment treaty.[19]

The chairman, Prosper Weil, resigned after appending a strong dissent to the jurisdictional award.[20] He had also chaired the *Banro* Tribunal and the arguments he presented in the dissent are familiar.[21] Weil drew attention to the specific object and purpose of the ICSID Convention – the protection of international investments – for the fulfilment of which the Convention 'prohibits the use of diplomatic protection and excludes the jurisdiction of domestic courts' in favour of ICSID arbitration.[22] Therefore, arbitral tribunals 'have to be particularly cautious when they determine their jurisdiction. An unwarranted extension of the ICSID arbitral jurisdiction would entail an unwarranted encroachment on both the availability of diplomatic protection and the jurisdiction of domestic courts.'[23]
Weil understood the purpose of Article 25(2)(b) to be the opposite of what the majority of the Tribunal expressed it to be. For Weil, sub-paragraph (b) of Article 25(2) was meant to recognize the reality of foreign investment under a national corporate structure:

It is this very same rationale of giving effect to the economic reality over and above the legal structure that should have led the Tribunal to decide that an investment made in Ukraine by Ukrainian citizens with Ukrainian capital – albeit through the channel of a Lithuanian corporation – cannot benefit from the protection of the ICSID mechanism and, as a consequence, to deny Tokios Tokelės, for the purposes of the Convention, the character of a 'foreign investor' in Ukraine. Since the object and purpose of this provision – and for that matter, of the whole ICSID Convention and mechanism – is to protect *foreign* investment, it should not be interpreted so as to allow domestic, national corporations to evade the application of their domestic, national law and the jurisdiction of their domestic, national tribunals.[24]

[19] *Tokios Tokelės* v. *Ukraine*, ICSID Case No. ARB/02/18, Decision on Jurisdiction, 29 April 2004, 11 ICSID Reports 313, paras. 53–6.
[20] Weil, Dissenting Opinion, 11 ICSID Reports 341.
[21] Schreuer seems to agree with Weil's basic position. See C. Schreuer *et al.*, *The ICSID Convention. A Commentary* (2nd edn, Cambridge University Press, 2009), 323, para. 849.
[22] Weil, Dissenting Opinion, para. 8. [23] Ibid. [24] Ibid., para. 23. Emphasis in original.

Weil accepted the corporate structure chosen by economic agents insofar as business law and issues of business liability are concerned, but:

When it comes to mechanisms and procedures involving States and implying, therefore, issues of public international law, economic and political reality is to prevail over legal structure, so much so that the application of the basic principles and rules of public international law should not be frustrated by legal concepts and rules prevailing in the relations between private economic and juridical players.[25]

In a more recent case, *Rompetrol* v. *Romania*, the respondent based its defence partly on Weil's arguments, since in that case the foreign investor was controlled by Romanian nationals, but the Tribunal rejected the argument: 'Professor Weil's argument had not been widely approved in the academic and professional literature, or generally adopted by subsequent tribunals. The Tribunal would in any case have great difficulty in an approach that was tantamount to setting aside the clear language agreed upon by the treaty Parties in favor of a wide-ranging policy discussion.'[26]

The *TSA* Tribunal reached a different conclusion, and argued that the situation was different under Article 25(2)(b), which allows the lifting of the corporate veil to determine foreign control. In this case an Argentine national had bought a majority stake in the ultimate owner of TSA. The previous ultimate controller was a Dutch company, and Argentina had agreed to treat the local company as a non-national. The Tribunal refused to stop the inquiry into foreign control at the first layer because:

It would not be consistent with the text, if the Tribunal, when establishing whether there is foreign control, would be directed to pierce the veil of the corporate entity national of the host State and to stop short at the second corporate layer it meets, rather than pursuing its objective identification of foreign control up to its real source, using the same criterion with which it started.[27]

[25] Ibid., para. 24.

[26] *The Rompetrol Group NV* v. *Romania*, ICSID Case No. ARB/06/3, Decision on Jurisdiction and Admissibility, 18 April 2008, para. 85, available at: http://icsid.worldbank.org/ICSID./.

[27] *TSA Spectrum de Argentina, SA* v. *Argentina*, ICSID Case No. ARB/05/5, Award, 19 December 2008, para. 14, available at: http://ita.law.uvic.ca/documents/TSAAwardEng_000.pdf. In a Concurring Opinion Arbitrator Abi-Saab stated: 'The establishment of "indirect" participation or possession necessarily implies the piercing of the second corporate layer (beyond the nationality of the host State). But if the text allows piercing the corporate veil to establish "indirect" foreign control at a third or fourth remove, could it prohibit doing the same in order to infirm this foreign control, by establishing that real control is in the hands of nationals of the host State?', para. 15(b).

The Tribunal recognized that other tribunals had not been consistent when dealing with this issue in the context of Article 25(2)(b): in *AMCO*, *Aucoven* and *Aguas del Tunari*[28] tribunals had refused to lift the veil beyond the first layer, while in *SOABI* and *African Holding*[29] they had lifted the veil well into the company chain. The *TSA* Tribunal, however, distinguished its case from the cases discussed by pointing out that in all of them the issue was the determination of the nationality of foreign control rather than its objective existence.

4. Misrepresentation

The question of misrepresentation was dealt with by the ICSID Tribunal sitting under the Energy Charter Treaty in the case of *Plama* v. *Bulgaria*. The case concerned the privatization of the Nova Plama refinery. In this case the Tribunal lifted the corporate veil, since it had determined that the real investor had misled the Bulgarian authorities in relation to the buyer of Nova Plama at the time of its privatization. A consortium – Consortium André and NOT – had been formed with the purpose of acquiring Nova Plama, but before the acquisition was completed the companies forming the consortium had decided not to pursue the investment. This notwithstanding, Mr Vautrin, now the sole investor in the consortium, continued to represent to Bulgaria the Consortium André and NOT without disclosing to the Bulgarian authorities that the consortium no longer included the initial investors, but only himself.

The Tribunal concluded that the investment in *Nova Plama* was:

> the result of a deliberate concealment amounting to fraud, calculated to induce the Bulgarian authorities to authorize the transfer of shares to an entity that did not have the financial resources and managerial capacities required to resume operation of the Refinery . . . this behavior is contrary to . . . Bulgarian Law and to international law and that, it therefore, precludes the application of the protections of the ECT.[30]

* * *

[28] *Aguas del Tunari* v. *Republic of Bolivia*, ICSID Case No. ARB/02/3, Decision on Objections to Jurisdiction, 21 October 2005, available at: http://icsid.worldbank.org/ICSID/.

[29] *African Holding Company of America and Société Africaine de Construction au Congo SARL* v. *Republic of Congo*, ICSID Case No. ARB/05/21, Award, 29 July 2008, available at: http://icsid.worldbank.org/ICSID/.

[30] *Plama Consortium Limited* v. *Republic of Bulgaria*, ICSID Case No. ARB/03/24, Award, 27 August 2008, para. 135, available at: http://ita.law.uvic.ca/documents/PlamaBulgariaAward.pdf.

The argument of reality versus form has been advanced both by claimants and by States, depending on whether the argument served the purpose of rejecting an objection to jurisdiction or defending it. There has been no consistency in the attitude of States or private parties in adhering to arguments based on form or substance. The positions taken by both investors and States have been guided by the convenience of a substantive or formal argument to the specific circumstances of each case. The tribunals' willingness to accept arguments of form over substance in relation to the nationality of corporations contrasts with the scrutiny to which arguments concerning the nationality of physical persons are subjected. For instance, in the *Soufraki* case the Tribunal rejected certificates of Italian nationality issued by Italian authorities, and commented that 'had Mr Soufraki contracted with the United Arab Emirates through a corporate vehicle incorporated in Italy, rather than contracting in his personal capacity, no problem of jurisdiction would now arise'.[31] Just the opposite of what Weil had argued in his dissenting opinion to the award in *Tokios Tokelės*. A commentator has wondered 'whether the mischief aimed at in cases such as *Nottenbohm*... is not broadly similar to the situation where an investor seizes upon a $100 shelf company in a foreign jurisdiction to use as an investment vehicle so that it might attract investment treaty protection?'[32]

Except in rare cases of fraud, tribunals have favoured the extension of their jurisdiction to cover corporations even if they are indirectly controlled by nationals of the host State, and even when intermediate controllers in the chain may not have the nationality of a Contracting State to the ICSID Convention. But how far removed can indirect control be and still benefit from ICSID jurisdiction? Some tribunals have recognized that the search for a link must at some point 'establish a cut-off point beyond which claims would not be permissible as they would have only a remote connection to the affected company'.[33] However, they have failed to establish where this

[31] *Soufraki* v. *United Arab Emirates*, ICSID Case No. ARB/02/7, Award, 7 July 2004, 12 ICSID Reports 158, para. 83.

[32] A. Sinclair, 'Nationality Requirements for Investors in ICSID Arbitration: The Award in *Soufraki* v. *The United Arab Emirates*', p. 2, available at: http://ita.law.uvic.ca/documents/CommentonSoufraki.pdf.

[33] *Enron Creditors Recovery Corporation (formerly Enron Corporation) and Ponderosa Assets, LP* v. *Argentine Republic*, ICSID Case No. ARB/01/3, Decision on Jurisdiction, 14 January 2004, 11 ICSID Reports 273, para. 52. In the same vein, 'La question de savoir jusqu'où le contrôle indirect peut aller a été examinée dans certaines de ces affaires. Comme le tribunal l'a fait remarquer dans l'affaire *Enron c. Argentine*, il y a lieu d'établir une limite à ce processus, car il risquerait d'aller tellement loin que même des investisseurs éloignés pourraient devenir des demandeurs protégés. Dans cette instance, la limite a été fixée

cut-off point is and have not offered guidance on how remoteness should be tested.

In this respect the certainty of who is the protected investor, from the perspective of the host State, has given way to protecting the investor's certainty. As the Tribunal in *Aguas del Tunari* held:

> the uncertainty inherent in Respondent's call for a test based on an uncertain level of actual control would not be consistent with the object and purpose of the BIT. The BIT is intended to stimulate investment by the provision of an agreement on how investments will be treated, that treatment including the possibility of arbitration before ICSID. If an investor can not ascertain whether their ownership of a locally incorporated vehicle for the investment will qualify for protection, then the effort of the BIT to stimulate investment will be frustrated.[34]

The policy of preventing the pursuance of investor claims through arbitration and through diplomatic protection at the same time – so vehemently expressed by the *Banro* Tribunal – has not been followed by other tribunals. The argument that multiple means of pursuing claims should not be followed simultaneously has been raised in some cases, but the respective tribunals have dismissed the question as one having merely a jurisdictional character.[35] The *Rompetrol* Tribunal refused to engage in 'a wide ranging policy discussion' to justify its refusal to consider the arguments expressed by Weil in his Dissenting Opinion in *Tokio Tokelės*, on which Romania had based its defence.[36] Policy considerations can hardly be avoided and, even if not discussed, they are implicit in the Tribunal's decision. Indeed, in *Rompetrol* the Tribunal followed a policy in support of its jurisdiction, even though the claimant company was under the control of nationals of the host State.

par le fait de savoir si le propriétaire et contrôleur indirects pouvaient être considérés comme couverts par le consentement que l'État avait donné à l'arbitrage, et il a été estimé que cela était effectivement le cas. Dans l'affaire *Banro*, la compétence n'a pas été admise précisément parce que le consentement donné par l'État ne pouvait pas avoir envisagé un demandeur d'une nationalité différente': *African Holding Company of America*, above, para. 100.

34 *Aguas del Tunari*, above, para. 247.

35 *Aucoven*, above, paras. 135–40; *ADC Affiliate Limited and ADC & ADMC Management Limited* v. *Republic of Hungary*, ICSID Case No. ARB/03/16, Award, 2 October 2006, available at: http://icsid.worldbank.org/ICSID/.

36 *Rompetrol*, above, para. 85.

4

Multiple approaches to define investment

The concept of investment is essential to determine whether the parties to a dispute have consented to arbitration and whether the arbitral tribunal has jurisdiction to hear the disputes arising from the investment. The term 'investment' is a recent addition to international agreements. As explained in a concept paper of the United Nations Conference on Trade and Development (UNCTAD):

> Customary international law and earlier international agreements did not generally utilize this notion. They relied instead on the notion of 'foreign property', approaching in the same . . . manner cases on imported . . . capital and cases of property of long-resident foreign nationals, where no transfer of capital took place or the original transfer was lost in history.[1]

How an investment is defined varies depending on the objective pursued: instruments concerned with the cross-border movement of capital and resources usually define foreign investment in narrow terms. In contrast, instruments directed at the protection of foreign investment use a broad definition of the term. This is the case of BITs, NAFTA, the Energy Charter Treaty, etc. The techniques followed in the definition may be different, but they coincide in their comprehensiveness or open-ended lists of examples to satisfy the objective of protection.[2]

The ICSID Convention does not include a definition of investment. At the time of the negotiations that led to the adoption of the Convention, there was no consensus as to the meaning of 'investment'. The absence of such a

[1] UNCTAD, *Scope and Definition*, UNCTAD/ITE/IIT/11 Vol. II (New York: United Nations, 1999), 9.

[2] Ibid., Section II.A.

definition in the Convention was not considered to be a major drawback by its negotiators. The emphasis placed on consent in the Convention meant that the parties could specify beforehand the categories of disputes they wished to refer to ICSID arbitration giving them, in turn, the possibility to specify what they understood as 'investment' for the purposes of ICSID. Nevertheless, the discretion left to the parties, as pointed out by Broches,[3] is limited and needs to be exercised within the objectives of the Convention. In other words, there is an objective limit independent from the will of the parties. Arbitral tribunals have recognized the existence of such limit, but there is tension between consent as the cornerstone of the Convention and the objective 'outer limits' of ICSID jurisdiction. This tension has become more evident in the context of the wide-ranging definitions contained in investment treaties referred to in the above. Some tribunals may distinguish between investment as understood under the ICSID Convention, on the one hand, and investment treaties, on the other. Other tribunals, however, do not carry out an analysis under both instruments, limiting their analysis to the definition under the investment treaty in question.

Whether or not an arbitral tribunal finds that an investment exists may depend on the choice of approach or combination of possible approaches. Should the approach be comprehensive? Should it be substantive or formal? Should the term 'investment' be interpreted broadly or restrictively? Should the elements used to delimit this concept be considered as jurisdictional requirements or simply serve as a guide to determine whether an investment has been made? Should the consequences of the investment be part of the analysis of the concept? These questions will be addressed consecutively and in the overall considerations closing this chapter.

1. The comprehensive approach

By and large tribunals carry out a comprehensive analysis of all the elements of the investment operation and consider 'the general unity of an investment operation', in the words of the Tribunal in the first ICSID case, *Holiday Inns* v. *Morocco*.[4] Nevertheless, there are exceptions to this approach. The

[3] A. Broches, *Selected Essays: World Bank, ICSID, and Other Subjects of Public and Private International Law* (Dordrecht: Nijhoff, 1995), 362.

[4] P. Lalive, 'The First World Bank Arbitration (*Holiday Inns* v. *Morocco*) – Some Legal Problems' *BYBIL* 51 (1980) 123, 159. The case was settled by the parties and ICSID proceedings discontinued. See also *Saipem*: 'In the present case, the entire or overall operation includes the Contract, the construction itself, the Retention Money, the warranty and the related ICC Arbitration', but it was not prepared to accept that by itself the

Joy Mining Tribunal insulated the guarantee of performance from the rest of the transaction and did not consider it part of the risk in view of the upfront payment the sale involved. Then it proceeded to dismiss the guarantee element in the contract because it considered that a contingent obligation could not be part of an investment.[5] But in fact, investments would often not occur if guarantees and other contingent obligations were not part of the bundle of rights which constitute the investment. The Tribunal was guided by the wish to limit what can count as an investment. But was it the right case to do so?

The Tribunal recognized that 'admittedly the Contract involves a number of additional activities . . . such as engineering and design, production and stoking of spare parts and maintenance tools and incidental services such as supervision of installation, inspection, testing and commissioning, training and technical assistance . . . But it does not transform the Contract into an investment.'[6] In relation to the guarantee, the Tribunal held that '[e]ven if a claim to return of performance and related guarantees has a financial value it cannot amount to re-characterizing as an investment dispute a dispute which in essence concerns a contingent liability'.[7] It is arguable that if the approach taken in *CSOB* or *Fedax* had been followed, this 'sale contract' could have qualified as a 'real' investment, irrespective of the form it took.

award was an investment, *Saipem SpA* v. *People's Republic of Bangladesh*, ICSID Case No. ARB/05/7, Decision on Jurisdiction, 21 March 2007, (2007) 22 *ICSID Rev – FILJ* 100, paras. 110, 113 and 127. According to the *ATA Construction* Tribunal, '. . . an investment is not a single right but is, like property, correctly conceived as a bundle of rights, some of which are inseparable from others and some of which are comparatively free-standing'. This Tribunal considered as a 'distinct' investment the right to arbitration, since it could hardly be considered as something other than a claim to 'any other rights to legitimate performance having financial value related to an investment', *ATA Construction, Industrial and Trading Company* v. *Hashemite Kingdom of Jordan*, ICSID Case No. ARB/08/2, Award, 18 May 2010, paras. 96 and 117, available at: http://icsid.worldbank.org/ICSID/. See also *Fedax NV* v. *Republic of Venezuela*, ICSID Case No. ARB/96/3, Decision on Jurisdiction, 11 July 1997, 5 ICSID Reports 186, para. 24; *Československa obchodní banka (CSOB), as* v. *Slovak Republic*, ICSID Case No. ARB/97/4, Decision on Objections to Jurisdiction, 24 May 1999, 5 ICSID Reports 335, para. 72.

5 *Joy Mining Machinery Limited* v. *Arab Republic of Egypt*, ICSID Case No. ARB/03/11, Award on Jurisdiction, 6 August 2004, 13 ICSID Report 123, paras. 41–63. See also *PSEG Global Inc. and Konya Ilgin Elektrik Üretim ve Ticaret Limited Sirketi* v. *Republic of Turkey*, ICSID Case No. ARB/02/5, Decision on Jurisdiction, 4 June 2004, 11 ICSID Reports 434, paras. 79–105.

6 *Joy Mining*, above, para. 55.

7 Ibid., para. 47.

In the recent award in *GEA* v. *Ukraine*[8] the Tribunal analysed each element of the investment individually, because the claimant asserted that a contract, together with a settlement agreement and an arbitral award related to it, were each by themselves an investment. The Tribunal rejected the argument in respect of the settlement and the award. It also dismissed the relevance of the *Saipem* decision on jurisdiction on which the claimant had relied, because the Tribunal in that case first considered as an investment the overall operation, which included a contract and, inter alia, 'the related ICC Arbitration, and then was not prepared to accept that the award itself constituted an investment.'[9] It is conceivable that none of the elements of an investment would severally qualify as such, but that they would in the aggregate. The *GEA* tribunal did not need to choose which elements to consider. The claimant did in the way it pleaded its case. What is important to retain is the need for the Tribunal to explain its choice of approach.

2. Form or substance

The form-or-substance debate remains unsettled, with both arguments enjoying the support of arbitral awards. On this matter, Schreuer has noted that '[t]he precise legal forms in which these operations are cast are less important than the general economic circumstances under which they are undertaken'.[10] Some tribunals have agreed with this opinion. Thus, the *ADC* Tribunal held that it was 'in favor of the Claimants' "*substance*" approach in considering [the existence of an investment]. Whilst attention need to be paid to the wording of the BIT with respect to "investment", the Tribunal believes it is the substance of the transaction that reveals the answer as to whether any investment was made.'[11]

[8] *GEA Group Aktiengesellschaft* v. *Ukraine*, ICSID Case No. ARB/08/16, Award 31 March 2011.

[9] Ibid., paras. 146–64. *Saipem*, paras. 110 and 113.

[10] C. Schreuer (ed.), *The ICSID Convention: A Commentary* (1st edn., Cambridge University Press, 2001), 138, para. 120. This sentence was deleted from the book in the second edition of 2009.

[11] *ADC & ADMC Management Limited* v. *Republic of Hungary*, para. 325. See also the award in *SG* v. *Dominican Republic*, according to which: '[a]s long as the business undertaken and the pertinent legal arrangements are lawful, as is the case here, there will be no reason to refuse the protections of the Treaty. This in the end is the reason why investment law has always searched for the economic interest underlying a given transaction and if it is compatible with the terms of the law and the Treaty, such interest is recognized

Other tribunals, instead, have disagreed with Schreuer's argument and with the *ADC* Tribunal, favouring a formal approach to the definition of investment. In *Berschader*, the Tribunal dismissed the argument that regard must be had to the economic reality behind the investments made by the claimant indirectly, and stated that 'such policy considerations cannot extend the protection offered by the Treaty beyond the terms agreed between the Contracting Parties'.[12] The dissenting arbitrator in this case pointed out that an interpretation such as that of the majority, which deprived the investors of the rights contemplated in the treaty on the basis of the corporate structure through which they made the investment, 'places form over substance and does not comport with the objectives of the Treaty'.[13]

3. Elements of 'investment': description or jurisdiction

To decide whether an investment qualifies as such, tribunals have interpreted this term on the basis of certain characteristics. Yet they differ on whether it is necessary for all elements to be present in the operation in question, and on their jurisdictional significance. The following elements,[14] part of the so-called *Salini* test, have been identified: (a) certain duration, (b) regularity of profit and return, (c) assumption of risk, (d) substantial commitment, and (e) significance for the host State's economic development.[15] This last element is not necessarily a characteristic of investments in general, but some tribunals have considered it necessary in cases under the ICSID Convention, on the basis that the Convention's preamble expresses the Contracting States' consideration for 'the need for international cooperation for economic development, and the role of private international investment' in this regard.

as entitled to protection': *Société Générale* v. *Dominican Republic*, UNCITRAL, LCIA Case No. UN 7927, Decision on Jurisdiction, 19 September 2008, para. 48, available at: http://ita.law.uvic.ca/. See also, *Antoine Goetz and others* v. *Republic of Burundi*, ICSID Case No. ARB/95/3, Award, 10 February 1999, (2004) 6 ICSID Reports 5, para. 89.

12 *Berschader* v. *Russia*, SCC Case No. 080/2004, Award on Jurisdiction, 21 April 2006, para. 148, available at: http://ita.law.uvic.ca/.

13 Ibid., Separate Opinion of Weiler, para. 14.

14 The term 'element' here is used in the sense of characteristic, what characterizes an investment for definition purposes, while in the previous section on the comprehensive approach, 'element' had the meaning of activity, which activities are included in the analysis of a specific operation.

15 *Salini Costruttori SpA and Italstrade SpA* v. *Kingdom of Morocco*, ICSID Case No. ARB/00/4, Decision on Jurisdiction, 23 July 2001, 6 ICSID Reports 400, paras. 43–58. See also *Fedax*, above, para. 43.

While some tribunals have religiously analysed whether each of the elements is present, others have taken an overview approach. *Malaysian Historical Salvors* and *CSOB* are examples of these two approaches. Beginning with the 'overview' approach of the notion of investment, the *CSOB* Tribunal inferred from the preamble to the Convention that 'an international transaction which contributes to cooperation designed to promote the economic development of a Contracting State may be deemed to be an investment as that term is understood in the Convention'.[16] In particular, and in relation to the so-called *Salini* test, the *CSOB* Tribunal noted that 'these elements of the suggested definition, while they tend as a rule to be present in most investments, are not a formal prerequisite for the finding that a transaction constitutes an investment as that concept is understood under the Convention'.[17]

Other tribunals have followed a similar line of reasoning. For instance, in *Mihaly* the Tribunal rejected the claimant's contention that expenditures made in the preparation of a future investment constituted an 'investment' for the purposes of ICSID arbitration in similar terms.[18] This general and reductionist approach appears to limit the notion of investment to whether the economic operation contributes to the host State's development and whether this contribution has been designed to assist in the economic development of the country.

The relativity of the concept of investment and whether the characteristics identified in the *Salini* test are truly differentiating traits become apparent in the following sample of cases where tribunals have addressed the elements of risk, a certain duration and a contribution, with various degrees of explicitness and thoroughness.

(a) Risk

Tribunals have considered the 'risk' requirement is satisfied by: (i) the length of the contract (*Salini, Bayindir, LESI and Astaldi*),[19] (ii) the uncertainty of the remuneration of the contractor, even if it is not linked to the exploitation

[16] *CSOB*, above, para. 64. [17] Ibid., para. 90.

[18] *Mihaly International Corporation* v. *Democratic Socialist Republic of Sri Lanka*, ICSID Case No. ARB/00/2, Award, 15 March 2002, 6 ICSID Reports 310, paras. 48–50.

[19] *Salini*, above, paras. 55–6; *Bayindir Insaat Turizm Ticaret Ve Sanayi AS* v. *Islamic Republic of Pakistan*, ICSID Case No. ARB/03/29, Decision on Jurisdiction, 14 November 2005, para. 136, available at: http://icsid.worldbank.org/ICSID/; *LESI, SpA and Astaldi, SpA* v. *People's Democratic Republic of Algeria*, ICSID Case No. ARB/05/3, Decision on Jurisdiction, 12 July 2006, para. 73(iii), available at: http://icsid.worldbank.org/ICSID/.

of the completed work, 'a construction that stretches out over many years, for which the total cost cannot be established with certainty in advance, creates an obvious risk for the Contractor' (*Salini*);[20] (iii) similarly, the price *à forfait* of the contract means that the investor does not know whether the result of the operation will be positive or negative (*LESI and Astaldi*); (iv) the nature and context of the work itself, like construction of a dam, implies risks and uncertainties related to the difficulty of the work, the nature of the terrain, the conditions of work and the modifications to the work to be performed that may be imposed or that may be necessary (*LESI and Astaldi*);[21] (v) existence of defect liability and maintenance periods (*Bayindir*);[22] (vi) the economic nature of the activity involved: an element of risk is 'implicit in most economic activities' (*CSOB*);[23] and (vii) the existence of a dispute as to the payment of the principal and interest of a debt obligation 'evidences the risk that the holder of the notes has taken' (*Fedax*).[24]

It is not evident that the factors considered to satisfy the risk requirement help distinguish them from the risks inherent in the performance of any contract.

(b) Duration

The long-term nature of an operation has been understood by tribunals as a characteristic element of investments that distinguishes them from ordinary commercial transactions under the ICSID Convention (*Salini, Bayindir, Joy Mining*).[25] However, 'long-term' has been understood as an elastic concept, and there are disagreements concerning the criteria for calculating the duration of the investment. The following elements have been taken into account by tribunals in the determination of the duration of an investment:

- in the case of *Fedax*, the Tribunal found guidance in the law applicable to the issuance of securities to finance the government's budget, without being concerned whether that would be too short a period under the Convention;[26]
- the period of the guarantee in the calculation of the duration of the investment, except in the case of *Joy Mining*, where the determination by the Tribunal that the contract in question was a sale contract overrode any other consideration;[27]

[20] *Salini*, above, para. 56. [21] *LESI and Astaldi*, above, para. 73(iii).
[22] *Bayindir*, above, para. 136. [23] *CSOB*, above, para. 90. [24] *Fedax*, above, para. 40.
[25] *Salini*, above, para. 54; *Bayindir*, above, para. 132; *Joy Mining*, above, para. 57.
[26] *Fedax*, above, paras. 42–3. [27] *Joy Mining*, above, para. 58.

- the fact that the payment was made upfront was not considered detrimental to the duration of the investment, except in *Joy Mining*;[28]
- the possibility of contract extensions;
- pre-qualification, only if not objected to by the other party, without the Tribunal raising doubts of its own on the idea that pre-qualification forms part of the investment; and
- duration is not affected by change of the investor: in *Fedax* the Tribunal considered the effect of the endorsement of the notes on foreign holders and found that: '[i]n such a situation, although the identity of the investor will change with every endorsement, the investment itself will remain constant, while the issuer will enjoy a continuous credit benefit until the time the notes become due'.[29]

(c) Contribution

A number of questions have arisen in relation to the contribution that the investment is required to make in the host State.

First, should the contribution be *substantial*? No agreement exists on this point, with certain tribunals accepting minor contributions and others requiring the contribution to achieve a certain threshold. For instance, the Tribunal in *Mihaly* noted that whether expenses are an investment or not cannot be determined in terms of whether they are large or small.[30] Similarly, the Annulment Committee in *Mitchell* considered that the contribution need not be sizable or successful to qualify as such.[31] On the other hand, in *Malaysian Historical Salvors* the relatively small amount of the investment was one of the determining factors in the Tribunal's decision that there was no investment under the ICSID Convention.[32] For the *Malaysian Historical Salvors* Tribunal the size of the contribution should be related to the host State's gross domestic product (GDP): '[w]ere there not the requirement of significance, any contract which enhances the Gross Domestic Product of an economy by any amount, however small, would qualify as an "investment"'.[33] But if such criterion is applied, the same investment may or may not qualify as such, depending on the size of the GDP of the host

[28] Ibid. [29] *Fedax*, above, para. 40. [30] *Mihaly*, above, para. 14(i).
[31] *Patrick Mitchell* v. *Democratic Republic of the Congo*, ICSID Case No. ARB/99/7, Annulment, 1 November 2006, para. 33, available at: http://ita.law.uvic.ca/.
[32] *Malaysian Historical Salvors, SDN, BHD* v. *Malaysia*, ICSID Case No. ARB/05/10, Award, 17 May 2007, para. 143, available at: http://icsid.worldbank.org/ICSID/.
[33] Ibid., para. 123.

State. What would qualify as an investment in Rwanda would not be such in the United States.[34]

The insistence on the presence of a substantial contribution to the host State's development measured in terms of the size of the investment may be misguided, as it excludes from the concept of investment certain small and medium enterprises which may not have substantial resources, but nevertheless have a significant developmental economic effect. Usually small and medium enterprises are engines of growth, and this is expressly recognized by the World Bank – of which ICSID is an affiliate – an institution entrusted with supporting 'the more useful and urgent projects, *large and small* alike'.[35]

Second, is the *timing* of the contribution relevant? In *Bayindir*, Pakistan had questioned the financial contribution of the investor because the price had been paid in advance. The Tribunal held that:

> The very fact that a part of the price is paid in advance has in and of itself no bearing on the existence of a financial contribution. In any event, Pakistan's contention overlooks the fact that Bayindir provided bank guarantees equivalent to the amount of the Mobilisation Advance payable to NHA 'on his first demand without whatsoever right of objection on our part and without his first claim[ing] to the Contractor.'[36]

In contrast, the *Joy Mining* Tribunal rejected that there was any flow of funds, since the amount of the contract had been paid at once at the beginning and the Tribunal did not consider it relevant that the guarantee was still in effect.[37]

Third, does the *origin of the contribution* matter? In *Tokios Tokelės* the Tribunal was being asked to narrow the scope of the Convention 'by adding a condition – in this case, an origin-of-capital requirement – not found in the instrument of consent or the Convention'.[38] The majority found that

[34] 'The monetary magnitude of investments cannot be accepted as a general restriction. It was considered but rejected in the course of preparing the ICSID Convention. Any State might of course adopt a policy of never giving its consent to ICSID arbitration with respect to investments below a certain magnitude . . . But other States may precisely want to benefit from the aggregate investment flows of attracting the small to middle sized businesses . . . This is their policy choice; not that of ICSID arbitrators', *Pantechniki SA Contractors & Engineers* v. *Republic of Albania*, ICSID Case No. ARB/07/21, Award, 30 July 2009, para. 45, available at: http://icsid.worldbank.org/ICSID/. See also *SG* v. *Dominican Republic*, above, para. 36.

[35] Article I iv, Purposes, International Bank for Reconstruction and Development of the Articles of Agreement, 2 UNTS 134. Emphasis added.

[36] *Bayindir*, above, para. 119. [37] *Joy Mining*, above, paras. 55–63.

[38] *Tokios Tokelės*, above, para. 80.

'neither the text of the definition of "investment", nor the context in which the term is defined, nor the object and purpose of the Treaty allow such an origin-of-capital requirement to be implied'.[39] The majority of the Tribunal was persuaded by the fact that the investor decided to deploy capital under its control in the territory of Ukraine instead of investing it elsewhere. The Tribunal affirmed that 'the origin of the capital is not relevant to the existence of an investment'.[40] It also found that there was no inconsistency between its findings under the BIT on the concept of 'investment' and the ICSID Convention. The considerations of the Tribunal on this point are intermingled with questions concerning the lifting of the claimant's corporate veil for purposes of finding the 'real' investor, a matter dealt with elsewhere in this monograph.

Weil, the chairman of the Tribunal, disagreed with the majority on the irrelevance of the origins of the investment's capital. In his dissenting opinion, Weil pointed out that the objective of the Convention was to stimulate 'a larger flow of private international capital into those countries which wish to attract it'.[41] He added that: 'The ICSID mechanism and remedy are not meant for investments made in a State by its own citizens with domestic capital through the channel of a foreign entity, whether pre-existent or created for that purpose.'[42] Weil's point is not off the mark. Consider, for instance, the hypothetical case of a foreign corporation raising funds in a particular State and then investing them in that same State. It is legitimate to ask whether this qualifies as *foreign* investment. Is it only the nationality of the funds' owner that matters? How does considering this a 'foreign investment' fit with the objective of improving the flows of foreign capital into the host State? While these may be valid questions in the abstract, they have been answered negatively by tribunals on the basis that the matter was considered during the drafting of the ICSID Convention and was dismissed by the drafters.

Fourth, is *preparatory work* a 'contribution'? The extent to which preparatory work may constitute an investment has been an issue in three cases. In *Mihaly* the parties never signed a contract and disclaimed any obligations arising from the preparatory work undertaken. Likewise, in *Zhinvali* the parties expressly acknowledged that the claimants did not have an

39 Ibid., para. 77. 40 Ibid., para. 80.

41 Ibid., Dissenting Opinion of Weil, para. 3, quoting *Report of the Executive Directors on the Convention*, para. 9, available at: http://icsid.worldbank.org/ICSID/StaticFiles/basicdoc/partB.htm.

42 *Tokios Tokelės*, above, Dissenting Opinion of Weil, para. 19.

investment.[43] In *PSEG* a contract was signed for the development of an electric power plant, but no plant was built. In this case the Tribunal took a wide view of investment and the significance of pre-investment expenditures:

> An investment can take many forms before actually reaching the construction stage, including most notably the cost of negotiations and other preparatory work leading to the materialization of the Project, even in connection with pre-investment expenditures, particularly when, like in this case, there is a valid and binding Contract duly executed between the parties.[44]

Some tribunals have added to the characteristics of investment the contribution of the investment concerned to the economic development of the recipient State. The issues raised by this element include but go beyond the question of whether the characteristics of what constitutes an investment should or should not be treated as jurisdictional requirements and deserves separate treatment in the following section.

4. Contribution of investment to economic development

In *Fedax* the Tribunal was satisfied that, because the promissory notes were issued under the Law on Public Credit, the transactions in the case were 'not ordinary commercial transactions' and 'involve[d] a fundamental public interest'. For the Tribunal what was important was 'whether the funds made available were utilized by the beneficiary... to finance its various governmental needs'.[45]

For instance, tribunals in cases involving civil works contracts have had no difficulty in finding that civil works were a contribution to the development of the country. Further, contributions to the development of the banking system of the host State have also been considered sufficient to satisfy this requirement, as evidenced by the *CSOB* award. More broadly, the *Mitchell* Annulment Committee has stated that: '[i]t suffices for the operation to contribute in one way or another to the economic development of the host State, and this concept of economic development is, in any event, extremely broad but also variable depending on the case'.[46] Yet the Committee found that 'nothing is said in the award about the content of

[43] *Zhinvali Development Ltd* v. *Republic of Georgia*, ICSID Case No. ARB/00/1, Award, 24 January 2003, 10 ICSID Reports 6.

[44] *PSEG*, Award, 19 January 2007, para. 304, available at: http://icsid.worldbank.org/ICSID/.

[45] *Fedax*, above, para. 41.

[46] *Mitchell*, above, para. 33.

the services of the "Mitchell & Associates" firm that would justify the decision to qualify them as an investment'.[47] The Committee recognized that some US investors had indeed consulted the 'Mitchell & Associates' firm. However, the Committee considered that the Tribunal's statement that it had received 'ample information about the activities exercised by Mr. Mitchell, including in particular the declarations made by former clients of the firm, the agreements concluded with former associates, and income statements . . . ' was insufficient and vague.[48] The Committee concluded that:

> The Award is incomplete and obscure as regards what it considers an investment . . . Such an inadequacy of reasons is deemed particularly grave, as it seriously affects the coherence of the reasoning and, moreover, as it opens the door to a risk of genuine abuses, to the extent that it boils down to granting the qualification as investor to any legal counseling firm or law firm established in a foreign country, thereby enabling it to take advantage of the special arbitration system of ICSID.[49]

While it is reasonable to assume that not just any services may contribute to the economic development of the host State, this case raises a fundamental question: which services would meet this condition? And more generally, how would their contribution be measured and at what time? Is the financing of a white elephant or the participation in its construction a contribution to economic development, or is it detrimental to it? How should economic development be defined for this purpose?

The *Mitchell* Annulment Committee considered that 'ICSID tribunals do not have to evaluate the real contribution of the operation in question.'[50] If the contribution to economic development of the investment is important enough an element for a tribunal to dismiss a claim if it is not fulfilled, it is legitimate to ask why tribunals should not 'evaluate the real contribution of the operation in question'. In his separate opinion as a member of the *Malaysian Historical Salvors ad hoc* Annulment Committee, Shahabuddeen defended the contribution of an operation to economic development as a mandatory requirement for the definition of investment. Further, he considered this element to be the distinctive feature of ICSID arbitration as opposed to commercial arbitration. If it were not for that, he wondered why States would agree to finance ICSID's budget,[51] and 'how a purely commercial entity, intended only for the enrichment of its owners and not

[47] Ibid., para. 38. [48] Ibid., para. 39. [49] Ibid., para. 40. [50] Ibid., para. 33.
[51] Ibid., Dissenting Opinion of Shahabuddeen, paras. 20–1.

connected with the economic development of the host State, is entitled to bring before ICSID a dispute concerning an investment in the host State'.[52] Shahabuddeen considered it possible 'to conceive of an entity which is systematically earning its wealth at the expense of the development of the host State'.[53] Neither of these possibilities was present in the case before the Tribunal.

In the *Biwater* case, Tanzania used the low rate of return of the investment as an argument to question the investment's contribution to its economic development. But the argument was misplaced. A low internal rate of return does not necessarily mean a low contribution to the economy of the host State. On the contrary, it may mean a low return for the investor, the opposite of the concern expressed by Shahabuddeen. Rather, from the point of view of the host State this could be an indication of the favourable business climate in the country. The Tribunal pointed out the difficulty in Tanzania's approach:

> Even if the Arbitral Tribunal had concluded that the project was a loss leader, it remains unclear why it should not then benefit from the protection of the ICSID Convention. Put another way, the Tribunal considers that if a party has ulterior motives for undertaking a project, and perhaps anticipates only a possible long-term and indirect benefit (e.g. other profitable opportunities), it thereby does not disqualify itself or its project from the ICSID regime. Indeed, the Republic's suggested approach would entail a difficult and possibly protracted investigation into the economic profile of any given project, as well as the particular motivation of those behind it, as an initial jurisdictional issue.[54]

In most cases the developmental impact of the investment concerned would not be known or measurable. At most, the contribution may be presumed on the basis of the character of the investment. Take, for instance, an investment for the construction of roads in the host State: it could be argued that in view of the character of the project itself it would be a contribution to the host State's economy, but it could also be argued that, from an economic development point of view, those roads may lead nowhere and constitute a misuse of State funds. The Tribunal in *Pey Casado* addressed this difficulty and viewed the determination of the investment's contribution to the development of the host State as a matter for the merits stage, rather than a jurisdictional issue:

[52] Ibid., para. 21. [53] Ibid., para. 22.

[54] *Biwater Gauff (Tanzania) Limited* v. *United Republic of Tanzania*, ICSID Case No. ARB/05/22, Award, 24 July 2008, para. 321, available at: http://icsid.worldbank.org/ICSID/.

An investment may prove to be useful or not to the host State without losing its quality of investment. It is correct that the Preamble of the ICSID Convention evokes a contribution to the economic development of the host State. This reference is however presented as a consequence, not as a condition of the investment: in protecting the investments, the Convention promotes the development of the host State. This does not mean that the development of the host State is a constitutive element of the notion of investment...[55]

The difficulty is compounded by different views on what constitutes development. The *Phoenix* Tribunal was of the view that such contribution was impossible to ascertain since:

there are highly diverging views on what constitutes development. A less ambitious approach should therefore be adopted centered on the contribution of an international investment to the *economy* of the host State, which is indeed normally *inherent in the mere concept of investment as shaped by the elements of contribution/duration/risk*, and should therefore in principle be presumed.[56]

The presumption may be reversed, and the award in the *Phoenix* case is an illustration of such reversal. The literature on development has pointed out for decades the lack of consensus in respect of the elements to be taken into account in a definition of development, and the weight that they should be given in relation to economic growth. It has also questioned whether it is appropriate for external agencies such as the World Bank to substitute its own views on the nature of development for those of a borrowing country.[57] This reasoning applies with more strength to arbitral tribunals, who should act cautiously in the assessment of the impact of an investment on the economic development of the host State.

Indeed, tribunals have failed to appreciate the evolving nature of concepts such as investment and economic development. Some have continued to judge these terms by reference to concepts that were prevalent at other

[55] *Víctor Pey Casado and President Allende Foundation* v. *Republic of Chile*, ICSID Case No. ARB/98/2, Award, 8 May 2008, para. 232, available in Spanish and French (originals) at: http://ita.law.uvic.ca/. The paragraph quoted has been translated by a committee member of the *ad hoc* Annulment Committee of *Historical Salvors*, above, Annulment, 16 April 2009, available at: http://icsid.worldbank.org/ICSID/.

[56] *Phoenix Action Ltd* v. *Czech Republic*, ICSID Case No. ARB/06/5, Award, 15 April 2009, para. 85, available at: http://icsid.worldbank.org/ICSID/. Emphasis in original.

[57] See, generally, E.S. Mason and R.E. Asher, *The World Bank since Bretton Woods* (Washington DC: Brookings Institution Press, 1973). See also this author's 'Investment and Economic Development', in M.A. Fernández-Ballesteros and D. Arias Lozano (eds.), *Liber Amicorum Bernardo Cremades* (Madrid: La Ley, 2010), 1033–46.

times, even though one of the benefits of the undefined concept of 'investment' is precisely the possibility to capture the new forms that business practices may devise. The difficulty of tribunals straying into certain fields unaware of how they have evolved is evident both in the contraposition of commerce and development and in the reluctance to accept legal services and cultural related activities as potential contributors to economic development. In this respect it is useful to contrast the dicta or holdings of tribunals on economic development, on the one hand, with how the World Bank has understood its activities in these three areas to contribute to economic development, on the other.

First, the support of appropriate trade policies and funding of trade facilities has been a feature of the World Bank's operations, which fall within its purpose to foster economic development. To consider the contribution of an operation to economic development as a distinctive characteristic of an investment, and to reduce it to purely commercial activities, presupposes that commerce is not a contributor to the economy of a State or to its development.

Second, and in relation to legal services, the World Bank has encouraged its borrowers:

> to address deficiencies in their legal systems which hamper the development process, such as the inappropriateness of laws (in terms of their failure to support the required policy changes and to introduce realistic incentives and remedies), ignorance of their content, uncertainty in their application, weak enforcement, arbitrariness in the exercise of discretionary power, inefficient court administration and slow and complex procedures.[58]

This encouragement has given rise to numerous initiatives covering the full spectrum of legal assistance: from law preparation to law enforcement; from support in the preparation of legislation to building judicial capacity and related infrastructure; from access to justice to qualified and affordable representation.[59]

Third, the World Bank was initially concerned that Bank-financed projects be located and designed to avoid, minimize or mitigate adverse

[58] Mason and Asher, ibid., 15.

[59] For an overview, see working paper on 'Initiatives in Legal and Judicial Reform on Legal and Judicial Reform' at: www-wds.worldbank.org/external/default/WDSContentServer/WDSP/IB/2004/03/01/000012009_20040301142827/Rendered/INDEX/250820040Edition.txt and, generally, the 'Law and Justice Institutions' website of the World Bank at: www-wds.worldbank.org/external/default/WDSContentServer/WDSP/IB/2004/03/01/000012009_20040301142827/Rendered/INDEX/250820040Edition.txt.

impacts on cultural property. In time, the Bank moved 'beyond the safeguard of doing no harm to assist countries and communities to conserve the most important parts of their past heritage and to embrace and celebrate their current diversity'.[60] This evolution is reflected in the benefits that need to be taken into account in the economic analysis of Bank-financed projects:

> The World Bank has always recognized that tourist revenues provide benefits that can help justify investments in conserving cultural heritage. This perspective remains valid, but *tourist revenues should not be seen as the sole rationale for such investments.* The *economic justification for investment in culture* must also recognize its *intrinsic value, its public goods character, and the positive externalities* that it brings.[61]

This shift highlights how culture has become integrated as an additional area which may justify financing by the World Bank based on its own developmental value.

* * *

This review of the different approaches taken by arbitral tribunals faced with the task of defining 'investment' evidences the difficulty to fix in a jurisdictional cast elements of this concept which are marked by their relativity. It also shows the perils of judging by consequences which are unknown at the time, or of ignoring the substance of a transaction.

The difficulties of the jurisdictional approach have been addressed by several arbitral tribunals. In the case of *Biwater*, for instance, the Tribunal considered the *Salini* test to be problematic if '"the typical characteristics" of an investment as identified in that decision are elevated into a fixed and inflexible test, and if transactions are to be presumed excluded from the ICSID Convention unless each of the five criteria are satisfied. This risks the arbitrary exclusion of certain types of transaction from the scope of the Convention'.[62] The *Biwater* Tribunal pointed out that the investment envisaged by the Contracting States in the Convention was left intentionally undefined and concluded that 'a more flexible and pragmatic approach to the meaning of "investment" is appropriate, which takes into account the features identified in *Salini*, but along with all the circumstances of the case, including the nature of the instrument containing the relevant consent to ICSID'.[63]

[60] *Culture Counts. Financing Resources, and the Economics of Culture in Sustainable Development* (The World Bank, 2000), Annex A.
[61] Ibid., para. 24. Emphasis added. [62] *Biwater*, above, para. 314. [63] Ibid., para. 316.

In the same vein, the *Pantechniki* Tribunal criticized the *Salini* test on the grounds that it left too wide a margin for the subjective appreciation of tribunals. According to this Tribunal, such a subjective appreciation had two limits clearly defined in the ICSID Convention: that the dispute be a legal one and that the dispute be between a Contracting State and a national of another Contracting State. These limitations should satisfy 'the notion that "consent alone will not suffice"'.[64] There was no need to establish a specific meaning of investment for the purposes of the ICSID Convention. According to the Tribunal, doing so would defeat the parties' purported consent.[65]

The difficulties inherent in making generalizations from the great assortment of factual situations that can occur show the wisdom of refraining from treating possible elements of a definition of investment as jurisdictional conditions which need to be ticked off a list. The relativity of such elements produces arguably greater uncertainty than the assessment of a transaction against the ordinary meaning of the term investment as analysed in its context.[66]

Some of the choices made by tribunals on the concept of investment have been guided by considerations based on the possible consequences of their decision. For instance, the *Mitchell ad hoc* Annulment Committee found that the inadequacy of reasons in the award would open 'the door to a risk of genuine abuses, to the extent that it boils down to granting the qualification as investor to any legal counseling firm or law firm established in a foreign country, thereby enabling it to take advantage of the special arbitration system of ICSID'.[67] The *Joy Mining* Tribunal, in turn, was concerned that if it found that an investment existed it would open the way for any sale to be considered as an investment.[68] Interestingly, the Tribunal's decision on the existence of an investment was made without taking into account the elements that the Tribunal itself had identified as differentiating factors of investments.[69] Further, in *Malaysian Historical Salvors* the Tribunal feared that, without a requirement of significance in relation to the investment's contribution to economic development, any contract could be considered

[64] *Pantechniki*, above, para. 40. [65] Ibid., para. 41.

[66] A broadly acceptable definition when elevated to a set of jurisdictional requirements introduces elements of subjectivity which '(a) transform arbitrators into policy-makers and above all (b) increase unpredictability about the availability of ICSID to settle disputes', ibid., para. 43.

[67] *Mitchell*, above, para. 40. [68] *Joy Mining*, above, para. 58. [69] Ibid., para. 53.

an investment for the purpose of accessing arbitration under a BIT so long as it represented an economic contribution.[70]

Justification by consequences is problematic because of the difficulty of projecting into the future decisions that are driven by the specific circumstances of each case. It may also be problematic in view of the lack of motivation of the choice made by the Tribunal among all the possible and foreseeable consequences. For instance, the *Malaysian Historical Salvors* Tribunal failed to take into account the well-known fact of the contribution of small and medium-scale enterprises to economic development and, as a practical matter, the unlikely rush of small claims, given the relative high costs of investor–State arbitration. Decisions which make contribution to economic development a peremptory characteristic of investments generally do not factor in the difficulty of determining what constitutes development, how and at what time to measure it, with ensuing uncertainty for the investor and the host State and possibly the inappropriate intrusion of the Tribunal in the policies of the host State.

The interpretation of terms such as 'development' requires an analysis of the evolution of the term and how it is understood at the time of the claim, rather than mere references to its obvious traditional meaning, such as the construction of a road or a dam. Culture and law may well contribute to development. Taking into account the great variety of elements such as these that may contribute to development is only congruous with ICSID's affiliation to the World Bank. Nevertheless, it is questionable whether a contribution to economic development can be used as a distinctive characteristic of the term investment under the ICSID Convention, particularly when the definition of investment seeks to distinguish it from commerce. Indeed, commerce may contribute to development just as much as investments.

The bifurcation of meaning of the term 'investment' under BITs, on the one hand, and the ICSID Convention, on the other, has the effect of denying Contracting States of the Convention the right to refer legal disputes to ICSID if they had defined investments too broadly in their respective BITs. Notwithstanding the certainty of this consequence, tribunals have failed to take it into account. One exception is the Tribunal in *Pantechniki*, which noted: 'One may wonder about the purpose of such denial. If the

[70] *Malaysian Historical Salvors*, above, para. 123.

words of the Convention nevertheless said so that would of course be decisive. But there is no such express limitation.'[71] It also has the effect of fragmenting the meaning of 'investment' under treaties entered into by the same parties, since most of the signatories of BITs are also parties to the ICSID Convention. The preservation of an autonomous concept under the ICSID Convention, independent from definitions agreed by Contracting States elsewhere, emerges as an objective valid by itself, irrespective of other considerations.

The denial that a transaction is an 'investment' through its classification as a particular service or a particular type of contract (a loan, a sale or a contingent obligation), without analysing the substance of the transaction or of the service provided, may lead to denying BIT protection on formal rather than substantive grounds. Further, these decisions are often made without providing reasons for the choice between formal and substantive considerations. The Tribunal in *Joy Mining*, having expressed its intention to delimit the operations that can qualify as investments, characterized the transaction in question as a sale, overriding other important elements of the transaction. This characterization entailed that the operation could not be qualified as an investment, even though the operation arguably could have been considered as such if all its elements had been taken into account. Indeed, the guarantee provided by the claimant was dismissed by the Tribunal outright and without reasons. The Tribunal in *PSEG* treated a similar guarantee in identical terms.

Further, different tribunals have assigned different weight to the various elements found in the preamble to the ICSID Convention. While an elaborate case law has developed around the term 'investment' and its relationship to economic development, the effect of the adjective 'international' added to investment has been largely ignored or dismissed. The origin of the funds for the investment, a matter of substantive concern in terms of actual investment in the host State and importantly related to the adjective 'international', has not been considered to be particularly relevant by tribunals who have dismissed its importance on the basis of the discussion that took place during the preparation of the ICSID Convention. It has only been considered relevant in relation to abuses of corporate form with the purpose of obtaining access to ICSID arbitration, but not in relation to determining whether an 'international' investment has taken place. The

[71] *Pantechniki*, above, para. 41.

drafters of the ICSID Convention may not have had in mind situations such as the one that the Tribunal had to deal with in *Tokios Tokelės*. The issue is not only a matter of manipulation of corporate form, but also of substance, whether, irrespective of form, there is truly a flow of funds into the host State.

5

Legitimate expectations, risk and due diligence

Most treaties provide for fair and equitable treatment and full protection and security as part of the same standard, some deal with them separately. This differential treatment is significant in the determination of the level of due diligence required from the host State to protect aliens during civil war, rebellion or disturbances and the relationship between the required level of due diligence and the country risk taken by the investor, on the one hand, and the level of protection that an investor can legitimately expect in such situations, on the other. In view of this important question, we will consider fair and equitable treatment and full protection and security as separate standards of protection. The chapter concludes with a section on BITs and the legitimate expectations that an investor may have under these instruments.

1. Fair and equitable treatment

The fair and equitable treatment standard first appeared in treaty practice in the early 1940s, and its content has been the subject of important judicial and arbitral case law during the last decade. But the standard has also been the subject of controversy, most importantly in relation to whether it reflects the customary law minimum standard of treatment of aliens or a higher level of protection. This debate has been considered sterile since the standard has to be interpreted in accordance with international law,[1] but this opinion

[1] 'The foregoing analysis exposes the sterility of the debate as to whether the fair and equitable standard of treatment is the same as the minimum standard of treatment for aliens in general international law. An international tribunal with jurisdiction over a claim based upon the conventional and general obligations would attempt to articulate a

seems to overlook the fact that at the root of the debate is precisely the lack of definition of the content of the standard under international law.

The determination of what is fair and equitable leaves a large measure of discretion to arbitral tribunals, which have used it to gradually build the content of the standard by applying it to the circumstances of specific cases. Thus the emerging content of the standard includes principles such as protection of the investor's legitimate expectations, transparency, freedom from coercion and harassment, procedural propriety and due process, and good faith.[2]

The concept of legitimate expectations has surfaced in the field of investment treaty arbitration in parallel to its appearance in other fields, such as human rights, European Union law, certain continental countries, English administrative law, or in employment cases of international administrative tribunals.[3] Unqualified reference to the protection of the investor's subjective expectations has prompted warnings both at the level of case law and doctrine. The *ad hoc* Annulment Committee in the *MTD* case warned that:

> The obligations of the host State towards foreign investors derive from the terms of the applicable investment treaty and not from any set of expectations investors may have or claim to have. A tribunal which sought to generate from such expectations a set of rights different from those contained and enforceable under the BIT might well exceed its powers, and if the difference were material might do so manifestly.[4]

The rise of legitimate expectations has been compared to the incantatory formula that acquired rights played in France at the beginning of the twentieth century. Such subjectivity is regrettable, because it seems to imply that the extent of the State's obligations depends on how the investor has understood them. It also invites the State to advance its own expectations.

particular conception of what treatment is required by both standards in relation to the particular circumstances of the case by drawing upon the same legal standards. These materials would inevitably include general and conventional international law relevant to the treatment of foreign investments': Z. Douglas, *The International Law of Investment Claims* (Cambridge University Press, 2009), 86–7.

2 C. Schreuer, 'Fair and Equitable Treatment in Arbitral Practice' *The Journal of World Investment & Trade* 6 (2005) 357, 373–4.

3 See generally, S. Schønberg, *Legitimate Expectations in Administrative Law* (Oxford University Press, 2000).

4 *MTD Equity Sdn Bhd and MTD Chile SA* v. *Republic of Chile*, ICSID Case No. ARB/01/7, Decision on Annulment, 21 March 2007, 13 ICSID Reports 500, para. 67. See also comments by Crawford, according to whom 'the expectations of the investor cannot act as a substitute for the relevant contractual and treaty arrangements', in J. Crawford, 'Treaty and Contract Claims in Investment Arbitration – 22nd Freshfields Lecture' *Arbitration International* 24 (2008) 351, 372.

The expectation of the investor to receive certain treatment is opposed to the State's expectation to freely conduct its legitimate activities. By themselves, neither the legitimate expectations of the investor nor those of the State allow the determination of the limits of the international responsibility of the State.[5]

For purposes of determining where the limit of the State's international responsibility lies in respect of the standard of fair and equitable treatment, I will review cases from the perspective of what is expected from the investor in terms of risk assumption and due diligence, in order for it to be able to seek the protection of an investment treaty.[6] Risk and due diligence are both related to country conditions, and in consequence they may affect the level of protection. These themes are interconnected and cut across all the standards of protection, but they are particularly relevant in setting the level and the interpretation of the standards of fair and equitable treatment and full protection and security.

Risk is inherent to investment. The assumption of risk by the investor is one of the defining elements of the concept of investment under the ICSID Convention, as it has been interpreted by arbitral tribunals. A bundle of risks are associated with foreign investment: business risks, country risks, regulatory risks, and so on. The issue is how to differentiate them and allocate them.[7] It has become common for arbitral tribunals to state that investment treaties are not insurance policies against business risks which should be shouldered by the investors as part of their business operations.[8] There are many examples of this: in *Fireman's Fund*, the

[5] E. Gaillard, 'ICSID Jurisprudence' *Journal de Droit International* [2008] 332–3.

[6] On due diligence, see generally, F. Lozano Contreras, *La noción de diligencia debida en derecho internacional público* (Barcelona: Atelier, 2007); C. Jiménez Piernas, *La conducta arriesgada en la responsabilidad internacional de los estados* (Universidad de Alicante, 1988).

[7] I. Brownlie, 'Treatment of Aliens: Assumption of Risk and the International Standard' in W. Flume, H.J. Hahn, G. Kegel and K.R. Simmonds, *International Law and Economic Order: Essays in Honour of FA Mann* (Munich: Verlag C.H. Beck, 1977), 309.

[8] See, e.g., *Salini* v. *Kingdom of Morocco*, para. 155: 'an investment protection treaty cannot be used to compensate an investor deceived by the financial results of the operation undertaken, unless he proves that his deception was a consequence of the behavior of the receiving State acting in breach of the obligations which it had assumed under the treaty', quoting *Consortium RFCC* v. *Kingdom of Morocco*, ICSID Case No. ARB/00/6, Award, 22 December 2003, (2005) 20 *ICSID Rev – FILJ* 391 (French original), para. 108, available in English at: http://icsid.worldbank.org/ICSID/. See also, *Joy Mining* v. *Arab Republic of Egypt*, para. 72: 'a basic general distinction can be made between commercial aspects of a dispute and other aspects involving the existence of some forms of State interference with the operation of the contract involved'. This Tribunal concluded that all claims were contractual and that the claimant had not 'credibly alleged that there was Egyptian State interference with the Company's Contract rights', see para. 82.

Tribunal denied the claim of expropriation and noted that the investor undertook an investment that was risky both in terms of the economic conditions in Mexico at the time and in terms of the specific financial institution that issued the Dollar Debentures that the investor purchased.[9] Likewise, in dismissing Waste Management's claim, the Tribunal referred to: '[a] marginal financial plan, predicated on a much more substantial federal guarantee than was eventually agreed, [which] foundered on the rocks of a deteriorating financial climate and a combination of little and large local difficulties.'[10]

This notwithstanding, it must be recalled that, since their early history, investment treaties have been closely associated with investment insurance schemes of the capital exporting countries that promote them.[11] Investment insurance may not be available unless the investment is made in a State which is party to an investment treaty with the State providing the insurance. Usually, under investment treaties a respondent may not assert as a defence that the claimant may request compensation for the alleged damages to an insurer pursuant to an insurance contract.[12]

Risk is also related to diligence. The level of diligence expected of an investor depends on the business risk and country context of its investment. Arbitral tribunals presume that the investor is an experienced and savvy businessman who has carried out adequate due diligence about the business

[9] *Fireman's Fund Insurance Company* v. *United Mexican States*, ICSID Case No. ARB(AF)/02/1, Award, 17 July 2006, para. 218, available at: http://icsid.worldbank.org/ICSID/ (redacted version).

[10] *Waste Management, Inc* v. *United Mexican States (II)*, ICSID Case No. ARB(AF)/00/3, Award, 30 April 2004, 11 ICSID Reports 361, para. 139.

[11] See E. Denza and S. Brooks, 'Investment Protection Treaties: United Kingdom Experience' *ICLQ* 36 (1987) 908, at 910: 'It was against this background of apparently eroding standards [those of the New International Economic Order] that the UK formulated its first Model Agreement for the Promotion and Protection of Investments . . . [in 1972] the Export Credits Guarantee Department was given statutory authority for the establishment of a UK overseas investment insurance scheme. Other States which operated such schemes linked insurance or at least supported their schemes with bilateral investment protection treaties. West Germany and Switzerland already had a substantial number of treaties in force. Experience in the context of across-the-board expropriations showed that these treaties stood up under political and economic pressures: German and Swiss investors secured the preference to which the treaties entitled them. France was also ahead with a number of treaties – mostly with former French colonies or protectorates. The US had agreements dealing solely with the technical question of subrogation – to ensure that when payment out was made under an investment insurance scheme the insuring authority could step into the shoes of the investor who had suffered the original loss. They would insure the States with which the US had a subsisting agreement.'

[12] See, e.g., Art. 10.20.7 of CAFTA.

and country conditions and how they may change, including how they may be affected by forthcoming political changes. For instance, the Czech Republic's introduction of stringent prudential rules for the financial sector caused distress in the banking system. In relation to these measures, the *Saluka* Tribunal found that the tightening of the regulatory system should be seen in the context of the Czech Republic's preparation for accession to the European Union, and it could 'hardly be disputed that these developments could have been anticipated in 1998'.[13] The same Tribunal presumed that the lack of effective mechanisms to enforce loan security under Czech law must have been known to the claimant when it made its investment and, therefore, an expectation that such shortcomings would quickly be fixed by the Czech legislature would have been unfounded.[14]

The presumption that the investor was able to foresee the effects of upcoming membership of the Czech Republic in the European Union (EU) was also applied in the *Eastern Sugar* case. There the Tribunal recognized that there was a liberal market for sugar made from sugar beet when the investment was made, but that this was not sustainable in view of the potential entry of the Czech Republic into the EU and of the regulated nature of the sugar market in the EU. It stated:

> That the market would remain free or would become even more free [*sic.*] could not be within the expectations of an investor such as *Eastern Sugar*. The wish within the Czech population to join the European Union was obvious. In 2000, an investor such as Eastern Sugar accordingly had to expect that the regulation of the sugar market would, as accession neared, become roughly the protectionist regime prevailing in European Union countries.[15]

Similarly, the Tribunal in *Parkerings* considered that 'an investor must anticipate that the circumstances could change, and thus structure its investment in order to adapt it to the potential changes of legal environment'.[16] At the time the investor had concluded its agreement in 1998:

> the political environment in Lithuania was characteristic of a country in transition from its past being part of the Soviet Union to candidate for the European Union membership. Thus, legislative changes, far from being unpredictable, were in fact

[13] *Saluka* v. *Czech Republic*, para. 358. [14] Ibid., para. 360.

[15] *Eastern Sugar BV* v. *Czech Republic*, SCC Case No. 088/2004, para. 236, available at: http://ita.law.uvic.ca/.

[16] *Parkerings-Compagniet AS* v. *Republic of Lithuania*, ICSID Case No. ARB/05/8, Award, 11 September 2007, para. 333, available at: http://icsid.worldbank.org/ICSID/.

to be regarded as likely. As any businessman would, the Claimant was aware of the risk that changes of laws would probably occur after the conclusion of the Agreement.[17]

In addition, risky situations, diligently investigated and assessed, may be considered business opportunities from which a businessman would wish to profit, rather than as mere country risk informing the basis of a claim for breach of the fair and equitable standard. The possible country risk is subsumed in the business risk because of the opportunities offered to the investor by the situation in the host country. The *Generation Ukraine* Tribunal found it:

relevant to consider the vicissitudes of the economy of the state that is host to the investment in determining the investor's legitimate expectations . . . The Claimant was attracted to the Ukraine because of the possibility of earning a rate of return on its capital in significant excess to the other investment opportunities in more developed economies. The Claimant thus invested in the Ukraine on notice of both the prospects and potential pitfalls. Its investment was speculative.[18]

The plea of the late Thomas Wälde that investment arbitration be distinguished from commercial arbitration and that investment arbitration should take into account the vulnerability of a small investor, as voiced in his Separate Opinion appended to the *Thunderbird* award, has not been heeded by arbitral tribunals. According to Wälde, commercial arbitration is 'a suitable mechanism for resolving the disputes of equal parties on equal footing and without need for the purpose of taking into account the position of the weaker party; nor is there any policy purpose underlying commercial arbitration'.[19] He saw his colleagues on the Tribunal as requiring 'a very high level of due diligence, of knowledge of local conditions and of government risk to be taken by the investor'.[20]

[17] Ibid., para. 335.

[18] *Generation Ukraine Inc* v. *Ukraine*, ICSID Case No. ARB/00/9, Award, 16 September 2003, 10 ICSID Reports 240, para. 20.37.

[19] *International Thunderbird Gaming Corporation* v. *Mexico*, UNCITRAL (NAFTA), Award, 26 January 2006, Separate Opinion of Wälde, para. 4, available at: http://ita.law.uvic.ca/.

[20] Ibid., para. 6. The size of a small investor has been taken into account in the determination of the site of effective management for purposes of establishing the link of a company with Singapore, in the first case under ASEAN: *Yaung Chi Oo Trading PTE Ltd* v. *Government of the Union of Myanmar*, ASEAN Case No. ARB/01/1, Award, 31 March 2003, (2003) 42 ILM 540.

These cases show that investors are expected to take the rough with the smooth before they can claim protection under the treaty.[21] The issue is, what level of roughness does the investor have to suffer before the breach of the fair and equitable treatment standard comes into play? It is accepted that the customary minimum standard of treatment of aliens has evolved and that States today would be held to a higher standard than that described in the *Neer* case. Pursuant to the *Neer* decision, there is a breach of the minimum standard of treatment of aliens when conduct of the State amounts to an 'outrage, to bad faith, to willful neglect of duty, or to an insufficiency of governmental action so far short of international standards that any reasonable and impartial man would readily recognize its insufficiency'.[22]

However, how much has the standard evolved since its first statement, and what its relationship is to the international minimum standard remain elusive questions, as shown by the interpretation of relevant treaty provisions by tribunals. For instance, when there is no specific reference in the treaty to the international minimum standard, as is the case in the BITs concluded by the UK, then fair and equitable treatment may be a higher standard, irrespective of the evolution of the minimum standard of treatment in general international law. Reference in the treaty to 'fair and equitable treatment in conformity with the principles of international law'[23] has also been interpreted by tribunals as supporting a broader reading that invites consideration of a wider range of international law principles than the minimum standard alone.[24]

To illustrate the uncertainty surrounding the standard of fair and equitable treatment, we will first review the level at which the tribunals have set

[21] Brownlie states that: '[t]here is no doubt that the thinking behind the evolution of classical international law concerning treatment of aliens was influenced by notions that the national venturing abroad should, within certain limits, take the rough with the smooth, and not treat his "home" government as a guarantor', in I. Brownlie, 'Treatment of Aliens', 314.

[22] *LFH Neer and Pauline Neer (USA)* v. *United Mexican States*, 1926, 6 RIAA 60. Brownlie considers this statement as expressing customary law. See I. Brownlie, *Principles of Public International Law* (6th edn, Oxford University Press, 2003), 503. See also J. Paulsson and G. Petrochilos, 'Neer-ly Missled' *ICSID Review – FILJ* 22 (2007) 242.

[23] See, e.g., Treaty between France and Argentina concerning the Reciprocal Promotion and Protection of Investment, 3 July 1991, 1728 UNTS 298; and Agreement on the Promotion and Reciprocal Protection of Investments between the Kingdom of Spain and the Argentine Republic, 3 October 1991, 1699 UNTS 202.

[24] *Compañiá de Aguas del Aconquija SA and Vivendi Universal* v. *Argentine Republic (Vivendi III)*, ICSID Case No. ARB/97/2, Award, 20 August 2007, para. 7.4.7, available at: http://ita.law.uvic.ca/.

the standard; second, whether the standard is considered to be an objective standard or whether it is subjective and, hence, whether country conditions are taken into consideration as part of the standard; and third, how the standard is applied. A separate section will deal with the extent to which that knowledge of the BIT may affect the legitimacy of expectations.

(a) At what level is the standard set?

Tecmed is possibly the award which sets the highest standard for fair and equitable treatment. According to the Tribunal, fair and equitable treatment is 'treatment that does not affect the basic expectations that were taken into account by the foreign investor to make the investment'.[25] Although this statement of the *Tecmed* Tribunal has been criticized for relying exclusively on the subjectivity of the investors, other tribunals have found the formula used to be easily translated into objective terms.[26] The *Genin* Tribunal, setting a lower standard of protection closer to *Neer*, said that 'acts that would violate this minimum standard would include acts showing a willful neglect of duty, an insufficiency of action falling far below international standards, or even subjective bad faith'.[27] This is the only award to refer to 'bad faith' to date. *Waste Management II* defined the standard somewhere in between these two extremes:

> arbitrary, grossly unfair, unjust or idiosyncratic, is discriminatory and exposes the claimant to sectional or racial prejudice, or involves a lack of due process leading to an outcome which offends judicial propriety – as might be the case with a manifest failure of natural justice in judicial proceedings or a complete lack of transparency and candor in an administrative process.[28]

(b) Objective or subjective standard?

In some cases a high standard is expected from the State without regard to its conditions. Thus the *GAMI* Tribunal, constituted under NAFTA, held that:

[25] *Técnicas Medioambientales Tecmed, SA* v. *United Mexican States*, ICSID Case No. ARB(AF)/00/2, Award, 29 May 2003, 10 ICSID Reports 134, para. 154.

[26] *LESI, SpA and Astaldi, SpA* v. *People's Democratic Republic of Algeria*, ICSID Case No. ARB/05/3, Award, 12 November 2008, para. 151, available at: http://icsid.worldbank.org/ICSID/.

[27] *Alex Genin and others* v. *Republic of Estonia*, ICSID Case No. ARB/99/2, Award, 25 June 2001, 6 ICSID Reports 241.

[28] *Waste Management II*, above, para. 98.

It is no excuse that regulation is costly, nor does a dearth of able administrators or a deficient culture of compliance provide a defense. Such is the challenge of governance that confronts every country. Breaches of NAFTA are assuredly not to be excused on the grounds that a government's compliance with its own law may be difficult. Each NAFTA Party must to the contrary accept liability if its officials fail to implement or implement regulations in a discriminatory or arbitrary fashion.[29]

Similarly, the *Eastern Sugar* Tribunal did not consider the circumstances of the country to be relevant in relation to the standard to be applied, and affirmed that it did 'not believe that for historical reasons the Czech Republic should be held to a less stringent standard than other countries, say the Netherlands'.[30]

On the other hand, after reviewing earlier cases that had followed the standard set by *Tecmed*, the *Saluka* Tribunal voiced its concern that if these statements were taken too literally they would impose 'inappropriate and unrealistic obligations' on the host State.[31] The protection could not be determined by the subjective motivation of the investor. Indeed, the investors' expectations 'must rise to the level of legitimacy and reasonableness *in light of the circumstances*' (emphasis in original) to be protected.[32] Country circumstances form part of the standard as such.

(c) Application of the standard

The application of the standard shows the Tribunal's balancing act between the relevance given to the level of country circumstances and the level of diligence or of risk to be taken by the investor. The high level of law implementation expected in *GAMI* was balanced by prior reference to the local courts as part of the standard, and not as a procedural requirement. The Tribunal recognized that GAMI had 'demonstrated clear instances of failures to implement important elements of Mexican regulations. It has adduced eminent evidence to the effect that the Mexican government is constitutionally required to give effect to its regulations.'[33] However, claims of maladministration could be brought before the Mexican courts. Something more than maladministration was required to breach the standard.

[29] *GAMI Investments, Inc* v. *Mexico*, UNCITRAL (NAFTA), Award, 15 November 2004, 13 ICSID Reports 147, para. 94.
[30] *Eastern Sugar*, above, para. 273. [31] *Saluka*, above, para. 304.
[32] Ibid. [33] *GAMI*, above, para. 103.

The *Generation Ukraine* Tribunal held the same view:

> it is not enough for an investor to seize upon an act of maladministration, no matter how low the relevant governmental authority; to abandon his investment without any effort at overturning the administrative fault; and thus to claim an international delict . . . In such instances, an international tribunal may deem that the failure to seek redress from national authorities disqualifies the international claim, not because there is a requirement of *exhaustion* of local remedies but because the very reality of conduct tantamount to expropriation is doubtful in the absence of a *reasonable* – not necessarily exhaustive – effort to obtain correction.[34]

It is uncertain how much of an effort would be required on the part of the investor to bring the case to the domestic courts of the host State. It is also uncertain what effect this would have where a treaty has a bifurcation clause whereby the choice between submitting the alleged grievances to the domestic courts or to an international arbitral tribunal is irrevocable. The Tribunal's view in *Eastern Sugar* that the Czech Republic should be held to the same standards as the Netherlands was balanced against the high degree of diligence expected of the investor, requiring it to have foreseen the changes in the protection of sugar production consequent upon the Czech Republic's joining the EU.[35] It was on this basis that some of the claims were dismissed.

The different degrees of protection by which tribunals have defined the fair and equitable treatment standard should be analysed in light of the specific facts to which they were applied. While *Tecmed* may be considered to uphold the highest standard of protection from an abstract point of view, the facts in that case may have justified a breach of fair and equitable treatment even if the standard had been set at a lower level of protection. Thus the uncertainty created by divergent definitions of the standard may be attenuated by the similarity of facts that have been considered to breach the standard, irrespective of the level of protection which is set.[36]

[34] *Generation Ukraine*, above, para. 20.30, emphasis in original. In contrast, see *Renta 4 SVSA et al.* v. *Russian Federation*, SCC No. 24/2007, Award on Preliminary Objections, 20 March 2009, available at: http://ita.law.uvic.ca/, where the Tribunal stated that '[t]he notion of actions before the courts of the host country are [*sic.*] problematic in principle. Courts are on the international level equivalent to other organs of the State. This means that the predicate of obtaining any amount of compensation according to any method would be hostage to the host State's self-determination as to whether it is due at all,' at para. 58.

[35] *Eastern Sugar*, above, paras. 236–7.

[36] See, e.g., *Vivendi III*, above, 'the difference between the parties may be more one of labeling rather than of substance. Significantly the parties find common ground in acceptance of the proposition that, in assessing whether the standard has been transgressed, a tribunal

2. Full protection and security

It is undisputed that under the standard of full protection and security the State does not have an obligation of result or of strict liability, as maintained by the claimant in the *AAPL* case.[37] Nevertheless, the level of vigilance required of the State may be affected by the nature and extent of possible revolutionary movements,[38] the habitual diligence of the State,[39] or the effective power over its territory of the State concerned, all of which indicates that the due diligence expected of it will depend on the weighing of facts.[40]

The relativity of the obligation of due diligence originates in the obligations owed by neutral States vis-à-vis belligerent States. The fulfilment of the neutral State's obligations was relative to the level of diligence that could have been expected of it, given a particular set of circumstances. It was often maintained that the scope of the obligation should be proportionate to the risks involved for, or the capability of the State. The *Alabama* Tribunal held that neutral States ought to exercise due diligence 'in exact proportion to the risks to which either of the belligerents may be exposed from a failure to fulfill the obligations of neutrality on their part'.[41]

But this statement of proportionality was not uncontested. In the *Salvador Prats* case, Commissioner Palacio interpreted proportionality differently. He maintained that the extent of the international obligations of a State must be proportional to the means available to the State to fulfil those obligations.

must determine whether, in all the circumstances of the particular case, the conduct properly attributable to the state has been fair and equitable or unfair and inequitable', at para. 7.4.12.

37 *Asian Agricultural Products Ltd (AAPL)* v. *Sri Lanka*, ICSID Case No. ARB/87/3, Award, 27 June 1990, 4 ICSID Reports 250. On this case, see S. Vasciannie, 'Bilateral Investment Treaties and Civil Strife: the AAPL/Sri Lanka Arbitration' *Netherlands International Law Review* 39 (1992) 333.

38 C. de Visscher, *Theory and Reality in Public International Law* (Princeton University Press, 1957), 278, referring to the conclusions of the US–Mexico Claims Commission, 1923.

39 Ibid., 280, 'the habitual or general diligence of the accused State counts for as much as its present responsibility'.

40 Ibid., 279, 'In spite of the accumulation of precedents, examination of the concrete cases reveals the impossibility of stating otherwise than in the most general terms the applicable legal criteria. Any systematization is to be avoided in a matter where everything in the final analysis depends on an exact and equitable weighing of factual circumstances which call for many and often very delicate distinctions.'

41 This is one of the Three Rules of Washington agreed in 1971 by the UK and the United States in connection with the Alabama incident of 1862, in J.B. Moore, *International Arbitrations* (Washington DC: Government Printing Office, 1898), vol. I, 653–4.

A State which uses all means available fulfils its duty irrespective of the result of the efforts.[42] This was also the opinion of Rapporteur Huber in the *Spanish Zone of Morocco* case: to require that the means used by the State 'always measure up to the circumstances would be to impose upon the State duties which it would often not be able to fulfill. Thus the view that the vigilance required should correspond to the importance of the interests at stake has not been able to prevail.'[43] Unlike Palacio, however, Huber seemed to recognize that there is a minimum requirement when he wrote that: '[a]s soon as the vigilance exercised falls clearly below this standard in regard to the nationals of a particular State, the latter is entitled to consider itself injured in interests which should enjoy the protection of international law'.[44]

It is uncertain where the intersection between capability and due diligence is and at what point capability or lack thereof would excuse the insufficient diligence exercised by the State. After an exhaustive review of arbitral practice and doctrine, the *AAPL* tribunal noted:

> the 'sliding scale', from the old 'subjective' criteria that takes into consideration the relatively limited existing possibilities of local authorities in a given context, towards an 'objective' standard of vigilance in assessing the required degree of protection and security with regard to what should be legitimately expected to be secured for foreign investors by a reasonably well organized modern State.[45]

This Tribunal judged the adequacy of the measures of protection in relation to the type of insecurity faced by the investment. The majority found that Sri Lanka had failed to take peaceful precautionary measures, prior to its counter-insurgency operation, to prevent the damage done to the investment. The dissenting arbitrator pointed out that the measures that the majority had maintained Sri Lanka should have taken were in fact inadequate, in view of the situation of civil war in the country. The conditions of civil war 'constituted an extraordinary situation which did not admit reliance on the type of leisurely police precautionary measures envisaged by the Tribunal'.[46]

[42] Moore, ibid., vol. III, 2893–4.

[43] *Spanish Zone of Morocco Claims*, Claim No. 44 *Rzini (Dar Ben Karrish, Harvest)*, 1923, 2 UNRIAA 615, at 716–17, translation quoted from B. Cheng, *General Principles of Law as Applied by International Courts and Tribunals* (reprinted, Cambridge University Press, 2006), 220.

[44] Ibid. [45] *AAPL*, above, para. 77.

[46] Ibid., Dissenting Opinion of Asante, 4 ICSID Reports 296, para. 4.

Further, the Tribunal did not consider the capability of the Sri Lankan police to take the adequate measures in question, possibly because its appreciation of the situation on the ground was less dramatic than that of the dissenting arbitrator. The Tribunal did not discuss the risk incurred by the investor by investing and staying in a troubled area either. But this issue was raised by the dissenting arbitrator, who doubted the causal link between government action and investment damage established in the decision of the majority. He further observed that the Tribunal's decision raised the question whether the investment losses were not due to the investor's 'continued involvement in the farm notwithstanding the overwhelming evidence of intense rebel activity in the area'.[47] Nonetheless, the Tribunal did take into account the effect of the civil disturbances on the expectations of the investor, and it excluded *lucrum cessans* from the determination of the quantum of damages.

As in *AAPL*, the question of the State's strict liability was also argued in *AMT* v. *Zaire*. In this case the Tribunal recognized that the obligation of protection and security of the investment was an objective obligation which must not be inferior to the minimum standard of vigilance and care required by international law. The Tribunal then addressed the question of what would be the practical criterion to determine the level of the precautionary measures to be taken by the host State to be consistent with such minimum standard. The Tribunal also raised the question of what would have been the appropriate measures to be adopted by Zaire in the circumstances to protect the investment of AMT.[48] However, it considered that it would be useless to enter the abstract debate of whether Zaire was bound by an obligation of result or an obligation of conduct, since Zaire did not in fact take any measure to ensure the protection of the investment in question.

If at first the choice of words of the Tribunal seems to suggest that the circumstances of Zaire were relevant in the determination of the measures that the host State could have been expected to undertake, in other instances the Tribunal appears to have had in mind that Zaire was under an obligation to meet an objective standard: 'The responsibility of the State of Zaire is contestably engaged by the very fact of an omission by Zaire to take *every measure necessary to protect* and ensure the security of the

[47] Ibid., para. 5.

[48] *American Manufacturing and Trading, Inc (AMT)* v. *Zaire*, ICSID Case No. ARB/93/1, Award, 21 February 1997, 5 ICSID Reports 14, para. 6.07.

investment made by AMT in its territory'.[49] But in the determination of Zaire's responsibility, at no point did the Tribunal address the question whether Zaire was capable of undertaking any such measure.

On the question of the amount of compensation owed, however, the Tribunal 'fully' took into account the situation in Zaire, a defendant that had pleaded throughout that no one could ignore that in the previous four years it had gone through a most painful and unfortunate period in its history. As the Tribunal in *AAPL* had done, the *AMT* Tribunal chose the method that 'would be plausible and realistic in the circumstances of the case' to calculate the amount of compensation owed, and in consequence denied the claimant's entitlement to *lucrum cessans*. It noted that doing otherwise would have served to 'enrich an investor who, rightly or wrongly, has chosen to invest in a country such as Zaire, believing that by so doing the investor is constructing a castle in Spain or a Swiss chalet in Germany without any risk, political or even economic or financial or any risk whatsoever'.[50] The attenuated damages were justified by the risky nature of the place of the investment. The Tribunal presumed that as a matter of course Zaire was inherently risky at all times, and in any case riskier than a European country.

Another feature common to the *AAPL* and *AMT* awards is the manner in which the respective arbitral tribunals interpreted the clause in the BITs limiting the obligation of the State for damages caused by war, insurrection or riots. Neither Tribunal interpreted this clause to be a special rule which derogated from the general rule of responsibility, and exonerated the State from the obligation of full protection and security.[51] An opposite treatment of the matter can be found in the *LESI and Astaldi* and *Pantechniki* awards. Both Tribunals in these cases proceeded to interpret the limitation on the State's obligation of full protection and security in cases of war or internal disturbances as derogation from the general rule of responsibility, deriving this conclusion either from the text of the treaties or from the level of diligence required of the State in such circumstances.

LESI Astaldi had claimed a breach of their security both under the standard of fair and equitable treatment and, separately, under the standard of full protection and security. Under the claim concerning the fair and equitable treatment standard, the Tribunal noted that the security obligation of the host State was an obligation of means and not an obligation of result,

[49] Ibid., para. 6.11. Emphasis added. [50] Ibid., para. 7.15.
[51] *AMT*, above, para. 6.13; *AAPL*, above, para. 65.

and as such it decided that there was no breach of fair and equitable treatment, since the security offered to the claimant was in proportion to what the State was able to offer and did not discriminate against the investor.[52] LESI Astaldi had also pleaded a breach of the obligation of full protection and security.[53] As in the case of *AAPL*, the *LESI and Astaldi* BIT provided in article 4.5 that in case of losses suffered as a result of war, armed conflict, revolution, revolt or state of emergency, investors would be treated like the nationals of the host State or of the most favoured nation.[54] Unlike in *AAPL*, though, the Tribunal interpreted the latter provision as a derogation of the general rule of full protection and security established in article 4.1 of the treaty and held that the two provisions could not be read cumulatively, since doing so would deprive the exception of any meaning.[55] The Tribunal recognized that the exception substantially reduced the protection afforded by the treaty and thus proposed a strict reading of the limitation. According to the Tribunal, the situation in Algeria after the signing of the contract was akin to a revolution, and the State had adopted security measures that could be considered reasonable and proportional, in view of the situation in the country and, in particular, in the region of the investment.[56] The Tribunal dismissed the claim.

In the *Pantechniki* case, the contractor had started to work on the project in 1994, and the events leading to the case happened in 1997. The Tribunal declared itself to have been impressed by the testimony of the project manager, who 'depicted in striking terms an environment of desolation and lawlessness which she and her team encountered upon arrival in 1994. The Claimant cannot say today that it felt entitled to rely on a high standard of police protection.'[57] It further stated that it was swayed by the project manager's testimony that the police were '*unable*' to intervene, which the Tribunal considered 'crucially different from a *refusal* to intervene given the scale of the looting'.[58] On this basis, the Tribunal concluded that the Albanian authorities were powerless in the face of the magnitude of social

[52] *LESI and Astaldi*, above, para. 154.

[53] The Algeria–Italy BIT does not contain a fair and equitable treatment clause; however, by use of the most favourable nation clause, the Italian investors benefited from the fair and equitable treatment clause in the Algeria–Belgium BIT. See *LESI and Astaldi*, above, paras. 149–50. The most favourable nation clause is contained in Art. 3.1 of the Treaty between the Italian Republic and the People's Democratic Republic of Algeria on the Promotion and Protection of Investments, available in Italian at: www.unctadxi.org/templates/DocSearch.aspx?id=779.

[54] Ibid., Art. 4.5. [55] *LESI and Astaldi*, above, para. 174.

[56] Ibid., para. 181. [57] *Pantechniki*, above, para. 82. [58] Ibid.

unrest, and dismissed the claim because of the claimant's failure to show that Albania did not comply 'with its duty to full protection and security in the circumstances that gave rise to this case'.[59]

In its decision on this point, the *Pantechniki* Tribunal also addressed the expectations that the claimant could have had when it entered the civil works contract. In the Tribunal's view, such expectations could not have been high, given the situation that the investor found in the project location at the start of the works in 1994, and were even presumed to be absent at the time of contract negotiation: 'An absence of such expectations may well explain the logic and value to the contractor of clause 11 of the Contracts by which the Employer accepted the risk of loss caused by civil disturbance'.[60] But this view of the Tribunal may be mistaken: the fact that the investor protected itself contractually from certain risks is evidence that it proceeded with diligence in providing for a future contingency, and not that the investor expected that the events against which it was protecting itself would happen. The investor's expectation would be that the host State would honour its contractual commitment. Yet in this award the contractual diligence of the investor is turned against him.

The BIT between Albania and Greece did not provide for an exception in cases of war, revolution or other internal disturbances. Nevertheless, on an argument based on the *consciousness* of State behaviour, the Tribunal considered that there was a difference between the level of due diligence required of the State in cases of denial of justice (a breach of the fair and equitable treatment standard), and that required in cases of breach of the standard of full protection and security. According to the Tribunal:

> A legal system and the dispositions it generates are the products of deliberate choices and conduct developed or neglected over long periods . . . A failure of protection and security is to the contrary likely to arise in an unpredictable instance of civic disorder which could have been readily controlled by a powerful State but which overwhelms the limited capacities of one which is poor and fragile . . . The case for an element of proportionality in applying the international standard is stronger than with respect to claims of denial of justice.[61]

The review of these cases shows that there is agreement that in situations of war or other internal disturbances the responsibility of the State under the full protection and security standard is limited, whether or not this limitation is expressly included in the BIT. The parameters of this limited

[59] Ibid., para. 84. [60] Ibid., para. 82. [61] Ibid., para. 77.

responsibility are determined through a proportionality test, which balances the measures taken by the State, on the one hand, and its capabilities and diligence in the use of the means available to it.

It can be seen how the determination of the diligence required of States in the fulfilment of their obligations of fair and equitable treatment and full protection and security has been dealt with in similar ways, as exemplified by the *LESI and Astaldi* award. Indeed, under either of the standards, the level of diligence expected of the State has varied depending on the circumstances of the case and the behaviour of the investor. But the 'sliding scale' of due diligence that may be expected of the State has a corresponding counterpart in the due diligence and the risks that an investor is taking by venturing into certain areas of the globe. However, the assumption of risk by the investor cannot be used as an excuse to exempt the State from responsibility where it has failed to take measures in proportion to the means at its disposal to protect the investor's operations.

The graphic expression of the sliding scale evidences the extent of discretion that tribunals have in finding the exact point of intersection between the due diligence required of the State and the assumption of risk by the investor. But it also evidences the difficulty of stating, otherwise than in the most general terms, the applicable legal criteria.[62]

3. Expectations and investor awareness of the BIT

Is knowledge of the BIT by the investor a relevant consideration for the determination of the legitimacy of its expectations? In *Lucchetti*, the Tribunal commented that the investor may consider:

> It a harsh result that its effort at obtaining an international remedy is brought to a halt before the merits of its contentions are even examined. Such a conclusion, however, would not be warranted in light of the fact that Lucchetti did not have an *a priori* entitlement to this international forum. It cannot say that it made its investment in reliance on the BIT, for the simple reason that the treaty did not exist until years after Lucchetti had acquired the site, built its factory, and was well into the second year of full production. It cannot conceivably contend that it invested in reliance on the existence of this international remedy.[63]

[62] de Visscher, *Theory and Reality in Public International Law*, 279.

[63] *Industria Nacional de Alimentos, SA and Indalsa Perú, SA (formerly Empresas Lucchetti, SA and Lucchetti Perú, SA)* v. *Republic of Peru*, ICSID Case No. ARB/03/4, Award, 7 February 2005, (2004) 19 *ICSID Rev – FILJ* 359, para. 61.

In *Jan de Nul*, the Tribunal used the existence of the treaty as part of its argument to distinguish that case from *Lucchetti*. It said that it was not 'undisputed that the BIT did exist when the Claimants made their investment',[64] but it did not consider whether the claimants had knowledge of it. When the State parties to the BIT limit the application of the treaty to disputes arising after its entry into force but do not exclude from its application investments made before such date, the consideration of whether the investor would have had the expectation of bringing a dispute to an international forum is irrelevant from a logical point of view – the treaty did not exist – and runs counter to the will of the State parties, which had permitted investments made prior to the entry into force of the treaty to be covered by it.

Yet the temporal element has been interpreted differently for purposes of determining whether the investor had engaged in the so-called 'treaty shopping'. In *Tokios Tokelės*, the non-existence of the BIT at the time of the investment was interpreted favourably in view of the inability of the investor to manipulate the nationality of the vehicle used for the investment in order to have access to an international forum.[65] Based on this fact, the Tribunal refused to lift the veil of the claimant, a Lithuanian entity owned by nationals of the respondent State, Ukraine.

In *Aguas del Tunari*, the Tribunal rejected as unfounded the allegation that the timing of the transfer of ownership of the claimant in anticipation of certain events which occurred three months later was fraudulent or constituted abuse of the corporate form. The Tribunal observed:

> a decision as to where to locate a joint venture is often driven by taxation considerations, although other factors such as the availability of BITs can be important to such a decision, and . . . it is not uncommon in practice, and – absent a particular limitation – not illegal to locate one's operations in a jurisdiction perceived to provide a beneficial regulatory and legal environment in terms, for examples, of taxation or the substantive law of the jurisdiction, including the availability of the BIT.[66]

The timing of a share transfer was also in issue in the *Cementownia* case. There the Tribunal recognized that 'treaty shopping *per se* is not in principle to be disapproved of, but in some instances it has been found to be a mere artifice employed to manufacture an international dispute out of a

[64] *Jan de Nul NV and Dredging International NV* v. *Arab Republic of Egypt*, ICSID Case No. ARB/04/13, Decision on Jurisdiction, 16 June 2006, para. 131, available at: http://ita.law.uvic.ca/.

[65] *Tokios Tokelės*, above, para. 56.

[66] *Aguas del Tunari*, above, para. 330.

purely domestic dispute'.[67] However, the presumption that treaty shopping is appropriate may be proven wrong. And the *Cementownia* Tribunal felt sufficiently strongly about this issue to state by way of *obiter dicta* that:

> Given the dispute's history and the temporal aspects of the case (a mere twelve days elapsed between the claimed acquisition of shares in companies already on notice of potential termination of the concessions and the actual termination measures themselves), had the Tribunal found that the share transfers actually *did* occur on May 30, 2003, it would have held that this case fell within the category of an artifice. Even if they did occur, the share transfers would not have been *bona fide* transactions, but rather attempts (in the face of government measures dating back some years about to culminate in the concessions' termination) to fabricate international jurisdiction where none should exist.[68]

The *Phoenix* Tribunal also found that the transaction subject of the dispute was 'not an economic investment, based on the actual or future value of the companies, but indeed, simply a rearrangement of assets within a family to gain access to ICSID jurisdiction to which the initial investor was not entitled'.[69] This Tribunal concluded that '[a]ll the elements analyzed lead to the same conclusion of an abuse of rights. The abuse here could be called a "*détournement de procedure*", consisting in the Claimant's creation of a legal fiction in order to gain access to an international arbitration procedure to which it was not entitled'.[70]

If BITs are to fulfil their purpose of promoting investments, then it is reasonable that investors should know of their existence and should take them into account in making their investment decisions, without such knowledge being assessed negatively by tribunals. Quite the contrary; that investors know and take into account their content should be a measure of the success of BITs to achieve their purpose. As reasoned by the *Aguas del Tunari* Tribunal, 'through the definition of "national" or "investor", such treaties serve in many cases more broadly as portals through which

[67] *Cementownia 'Nowa Huta' SA* v. *Republic of Turkey*, ICSID Case No. ARB(AF)/06/2 (ECT), Award, 17 September 2009, para. 117, available at: http://ita.law.uvic.ca/.

[68] Ibid. The Tribunal felt this way notwithstanding the fact that '[t]he Claimant was frank about the reasoning underlying its claim. According to Mr. Uzan, he transferred the shares because he feared that "the government would unilaterally take at least the transmission rights of the companies" and he "wanted to protect our interests" (Kemal Uzan witness statement, para. 32)'. The way in which he claimed to have protected his interests was to transfer his shares to a foreign company that his family's company, the Rumeli Group, in turn controlled. See at para. 116.

[69] *Phoenix*, above, para. 140.

[70] Ibid., para. 143. See also *SG* v. *Dominican Republic*, above, para. 110.

investments are structured, organized, and, most importantly, encouraged through the availability of a neutral forum'.[71]

To the extent that BITs are used as instruments to compete for foreign investment, treaty shopping is a consequence of comparing different investment regimes. The neutral forum offered in those treaties could equally be provided through domestic legislation, as is the case in certain countries. The negative connotation that seems inherent in the expression 'treaty shopping' would not seem apposite to search for the most friendly domestic investment regime. Yet any right can be subject to abuse, and the circumstances in which such abuses occur should be carefully evaluated by tribunals.

[71] *Aguas del Tunari* above, para. 332. Footnote omitted.

Part III

The search for consistency

Introduction

Different views on points of law and contradictory decisions on the basis of the same or similar factual situations prompted calls for an appeals mechanism. So far this idea has not prospered. However, the need for consistency remains 'for the sake of the development of the rule of law'.[1] It is the purpose of this part to explore the extent to which principles, precedents and publicists contribute to consistency in investment treaty arbitration.

[1] G. Kaufmann-Kohler, 'Is Consistency a Myth?', in E. Gaillard and Y. Banifatemi (eds.), *Precedent in International Arbitration* (New York: Juris Publishing, 2008), 145. See the extensive literature on this topic referred to in that chapter and the recently published G. Guillaume, 'The Use of Precedent by International Judges and Arbitrators' *Journal of International Dispute Settlement* 2 (2011) 5–23.

6

Principles

In international law the term 'principle' is used rather loosely. At times it is understood as an equivalent to 'rules',[1] whereas at other times 'rules' include 'principles'. In its ordinary meaning the term 'principle' refers to a general norm which explains and justifies more specific rules.[2] Article 31(3)(c) of the Vienna Convention requires that in the interpretation of treaties a treaty interpreter take into account the context of the treaty, together with '[a]ny relevant rules of international law applicable in the relations between the parties'.[3] The *Report of the Study Group of the International Law Commission on the Fragmentation of International Law* referred to article 31(3)(c) as embodying a principle of systemic integration and considered it to cover all the sources of international law, including custom, general principles of law and, where applicable, other treaties.[4] The *Fragmentation Report* incorporated under 'rules' the term 'principles' and noted

[1] The French version of the ICSID Convention uses the term 'principles' in Article 42(1) on applicable law, while the Spanish and English versions of that article use the terms 'norms' and 'rules', respectively. The ICJ itself has used the terms 'rule' and 'principle' indistinctly in the same paragraph in respect of the exhaustion of local remedies: 'the parties to a treaty can therein either agree that the *local remedies rule* should apply to claims based on alleged breaches of that treaty; or confirm that it shall apply. Yet the Chamber finds itself unable to accept that an important *principle of customary international law* could be held to have been tacitly dispensed with, in the absence of any words making clear the intention to do so', *Elettronica Sicula SPA (ELSI)*, Judgment, ICJ Reports 1989, 15, 42 (para. 50). (Emphasis added.)

[2] N. MacCormick, *Legal Reasoning and Legal Theory* (Oxford University Press, 1979), 152.

[3] Vienna Convention on the Law of Treaties, 23 May 1969, 1155 UNTS 331.

[4] See ILC, *Report of the Study Group on Fragmentation of International Law: Difficulties arising from the Diversification and Expansion of International Law*, 13 April 2006, A/CN.4/L.682, Part F, 206 (para. 426.b), Hereinafter 'Fragmentation Report'. See also, C. Mclachlan, 'Principle of Systemic Integration and Article 31(3)(c) of the Vienna Convention' *ICLQ* 54 (2005) 279.

that these two terms are used indistinctly, and not in their technical sense, by tribunals and in State practice. Similarly, investment treaties contain references to both 'principles of international law' and 'international law'.[5]

That a treaty as an international law instrument needs to be interpreted in accordance with international law, including the general principles of law, was well accepted in the practice of tribunals even before the entry into force of the Vienna Convention on the Law of Treaties. The matter was considered so obvious that the European Convention on Human Rights lacks an equivalent provision to Article 38(1)(c) of the Statute of the ICJ.[6] This omission was 'quite deliberate, not because those responsible for producing the Convention wished to withhold access to general principles from those entrusted with its interpretation, but, on the contrary, because they saw the use of general principles as inevitable.'[7]

There is no general agreement on what is meant by Article 38(1)(c).[8] Principles have been understood as a distillation of essential notions found in municipal laws or as principles of natural law.[9] One opinion holds that:

> The expression 'general principles of law' does not imply generalizations reached by application of comparative law and abstract legal science (although that is not to be excluded and is frequently met in individual judicial opinions). It refers more to the particularization of an underlying sense of what is just in the circumstances.[10]

While another view considers that '[g]eneral principles of law are not an expression of general feelings of justice or equity but are part of the body of international law which, in a particular case, must be proven and not

5 For differences in wording of investment treaties see A. Newcombe and L. Paradell, *Law Practice of Investment Treaties. Standards of Treatment* (The Netherlands: Kluwer Law International, 2009), 79 ff.

6 European Convention for the Protection of Human Rights and Fundamental Freedoms, 11 April 1950, 213 UNTS 222; Statute of the International Court of Justice, 26 June 1945, 33 UNTS 993.

7 M.J.G. Merrils, *The Development of International Law by the European Court of Human Rights* (2nd edn, Manchester University Press, 1993), 177.

8 R.Y. Jennings, 'General Course on Principles of International Law' *Recueil* 121 (1967) 323, 338.

9 Ibid., 339. In fact, Article 38(1)(c) was intended to be a compromise between these two positions.

10 S. Rosenne, 'General Course on Public International Law' *Recueil des cours* 291 (2001), 63–4.

presumed'.[11] This notwithstanding, Article 38(1)(c) assumes the essential unity of all law and enables 'apparent gaps and weak places in the law to be turned to account as opportunities for progressive development'.[12]

Principles are sometimes considered in opposition to policies, such as the policies referred to in the preambles to investment treaties. It is argued that it is not the role of tribunals to decide a dispute on the basis of such policies, but on the basis of principles.[13] This argument relies on the distinction between principles and policies advanced by Dworkin, according to whom principles are 'a standard that is to be observed, not because it will advance or secure an economic, political, or social situation deemed desirable, but because it is a requirement of justice or fairness or some other dimension of morality'. Policies, on the other hand, are 'that kind of standard that sets out a goal to be reached, generally an improvement in some economic, political, or social feature of the community'.[14]

But Dworkin's position has been criticized on two levels. First, he has been criticized for labelling his preferred policies 'principles', and for urging 'judges to decide cases in accordance with those "principles" and ignore (other) "policies", which are consigned to the legislature'.[15] Second, and on a higher level of abstraction, it has been maintained that the distinction between principles and policies may not, however, be so clear:

[11] C. Schreuer *et al.*, *The ICSID Convention: A Commentary* (2nd edn, Cambridge University Press, 2009), 610. See also discussion of the various views in B. Cheng, *General Principles of Law as Applied by International Courts and Tribunals* (Cambridge University Press, 2006), 2 ff.

[12] Jennings, 'General Course on Principles of International Law', 340. He considers that 'the provision [Article 38(1)(c)] is a salutary addition to Article 38 if employed with caution. It is not so much a defect as a virtue in a provision of this kind that it is possible to understand it in different ways.' J.L. Brierly calls it 'an authoritative recognition of a dynamic element in international law', in *The Law of Nations* (6th edn, rev. C.H.M. Waldock, Oxford: Clarendon Press, 1963), 63.

[13] 'to invoke a policy based upon the preambular statements to resolve a concrete dispute is often to substitute speculative discourse for principled arguments', Z. Douglas, *The International Law of Investment Claims*, 84. The same author states that: 'The collective goals that motivated the contracting states to conclude an investment treaty, as articulated in its preamble, cannot be decisive in the tribunal's resolution of conflicting assertions of individuated rights. Where there is no specific rule of decision to apply, which is invariably the case in investment treaty arbitration, the tribunal should search for principles of law. For instance, a tribunal would be on safer ground by making reference to the principle of estoppel or legitimate expectations to give content to the fair and equitable standard of treatment, rather than appealing to the policy of achieving "greater economic cooperation" between the contracting states to the treaty', ibid.

[14] Quoted in ibid., 83.

[15] R. Posner, *How Judges Think* (Cambridge, Mass.: Harvard University Press, 2008), 175.

when in law or in any other sphere we raise the question whether a given policy goal is desirable or not, we are raising a question of principle. For any goal *g*, to say that it is a goal which *ought* to be secured is to enunciate a principle or a judgment dependent on some unstated but presupposed principle. For this reason, the spheres of principle and of policy are not distinct and mutually opposed but irretrievably interlocking.[16]

General principles of law have been important in areas of the law which involve non-State actors, such as investment relationships and arbitrations between States and foreign nationals.[17] While the ICJ seldom refers to general principles of law, 'other international courts have been rather more proactive than the ICJ, perhaps because of their greater need to respond to contemporary demands'.[18] This is the case in investment treaty arbitrations,[19] where general principles may exercise a unifying function in the interpretation of the general standards of treatment provided for in investment treaties. Further, there may be room for a larger role for principles extracted from the judicial review of public decisions in municipal legal systems.[20]

This part will review decisions of arbitral tribunals in which general principles of law have produced a consistent result, decisions where principles have been used to integrate a particular interpretation in the wider context of international law and decisions where opposite principles were applicable and consistency elusive.

In cases concerning corruption, fraud and misrepresentation tribunals have often relied on the principle of good faith (linked in multiple ways to the concept of international public policy), which has then played an important unifying role in the interpretation of the treaties in question and has led to the adoption of consistent decisions by different tribunals on the basis of similar facts. In the case of *Inceysa*, where a Spanish company brought a claim against the Salvadoran government for contractual breaches and expropriation, the BIT between El Salvador and Spain required the Tribunal to decide disputes in accordance with 'generally recognized rules and principles of International Law'.[21] The Tribunal proceeded by referring to

16 MacCormick, *Legal Reasoning and Legal Theory*, 265.
17 Schreuer *et al.*, *The ICSID Convention*, 608.
18 C. Chinkin and A. Boyle, *The Making of International Law* (Oxford University Press, 2007), 286.
19 For a list of principles and cases, see Schreuer *et al.*, *The ICSID Convention*, 608–9.
20 Douglas, *The International Law of Investment Claims*, 89.
21 Agreement Between the Kingdom of Spain and the Republic of El Salvador on the Reciprocal Promotion and Protection of Investments, 14 February 1995, 1933 UNTS 363, Article XI (para. 3).

Article 38 of the ICJ Statute and noted that general principles of law had been understood 'as general rules on which there is international consensus to consider them as universal standards and rules of conduct that must always be applied and which, in the opinion of important commentators are rules of law on which the legal systems of States are based'.[22] Based on this understanding, the Tribunal considered the principles of good faith, *nemo auditor propriam turpitudinem allegans* and international public policy and found the claimant to have been in breach of all of these principles.

Good faith was violated by the claimant's presentation of false financial information as part of its tender, by its making false representations in respect of its experience and capacity to comply with the terms of the contract in question, and by its falsifying documents and covering up a relationship with another bidder. According to the Tribunal, since Inceysa had acted improperly in order to win the bid, its investment could not 'be given [the] protection granted by the BIT. Sustaining the contrary would be to violate the aforementioned general principles of law which . . . are part of Salvadoran law.'[23] For the Tribunal, the inclusion of the expression 'in accordance with law' in several clauses of the investment treaty was a clear manifestation of international policy which the Tribunal understood to consist of 'a series of fundamental principles that constitute[d] the very essence of the State' and whose 'essential function [was] to preserve the values of the international legal system against actions contrary to it'.[24]

In *Plama*, the Tribunal found that the investment was obtained by deceit in violation of Bulgarian law and that granting the protection of the Energy Charter Treaty to the investment would run counter to the principle *nemo auditor propriam turpitudinem allegans* and 'the basic notion of international public policy – that a contract obtained by wrongful means (fraudulent misrepresentation) should not be enforced by a tribunal'.[25] In the Tribunal's view, the principle of good faith encompassed the obligation of the investor to provide the host State with relevant and material information concerning the investor and the investment, where that information was necessary for the State's approval of the investment.[26]

[22] *Inceysa Vallisoletana SL* v. *Republic of El Salvador*, ICSID Case No. ARB/03/26, Award, 2 August 2006, para. 227, available at: http://ita.law.uvic.ca/documents/Inceysa_Vallisoletana_en_001.pdf.

[23] Ibid., para. 243. [24] Ibid., paras. 245–6.

[25] *Plama Consortium Limited* v. *Republic of Bulgaria*, ICSID Case No. ARB/03/24, Award, 27 August 2008, para. 143, available at: http://ita.law.uvic.ca/documents/PlamaBulgariaAward.pdf.

[26] Ibid., para. 144.

In *World Duty Free* v. *Kenya*, the Tribunal appealed to 'international public policy', which it understood to mean 'an international consensus on universal standards and accepted norms of conduct that must be applied in all fora'.[27] It stressed that tribunals must be very cautious and 'carefully check the objective existence of a particular transnational public policy rule in identifying it through international conventions, comparative law and arbitral awards.'[28] In this respect, the Tribunal noted that bribery or influence peddling was sanctioned by criminal law in most, if not all, countries, including Kenya. Further, it noted that a number of international conventions had been concluded at the regional level, including Africa, and at worldwide level, and that Kenya had ratified both the African convention and the convention prepared under UN auspices. While the Tribunal recognized that conventions are binding only on the State parties, 'States have shown their common will to fight corruption, not only through national legislation, as they did before, but also through international cooperation. In doing so, States not only reached a new stage in the fight against corruption, but also solidly confirmed their prior condemnation of it.'[29] The Tribunal then referred to the practice of domestic courts and arbitral tribunals and concluded that:

> In light of domestic laws and international conventions relating to corruption, and in light of the decisions taken in this matter by courts and arbitral tribunals, this Tribunal is convinced that bribery is contrary to the international public policy of most, if not all, States or, to use another formula, to transnational public policy. Thus, claims based on contracts of corruption or on contracts obtained by corruption cannot be upheld by this Arbitral Tribunal.[30]

The *Phoenix* Tribunal analysed the ICSID Convention and the BIT with due regard to the requirements of the general principles of law which could not:

> be read and interpreted in isolation from public international law, and its general principles. To take an extreme example, nobody would suggest that ICSID protection should be granted to investments made in violation of the most fundamental

[27] *World Duty Free Company* v. *Republic of Kenya*, ICSID Case No. ARB/00/7, Award, 4 October 2006, para. 139, available at: http://ita.law.uvic.ca/documents/WDFv.KenyaAward.pdf.

[28] Ibid., para. 141, quoting, E. Gaillard, 'Trente ans de *Lex Mercatoria* – Pour une application sélective de la méthode des principes généraux de droit' *Journal du droit international* 122 (1995) 5.

[29] *World Duty Free*, para. 148. [30] Ibid., para. 157.

rules of protection of human rights, like investments made in pursuance of torture or genocide or in support of slavery or trafficking of human organs.[31]

In this case, the objective of the Tribunal was to 'ensure that the ICSID mechanism does not protect investments that it was not designed to protect, because they are in essence domestic investments disguised as international investments for the sole purpose of access to this mechanism'.[32] The Tribunal relied on the principle of good faith, which it considered as a 'kind of "Janus concept", with one face looking at the national legal order and one at the international legal order',[33] and pointed out that this principle had 'long been recognized in public international law and in all national legal systems' and that it governed 'the legal rights and duties of those seeking to assert an international claim under a treaty'.[34] The *Phoenix* Tribunal concluded that the investment was not a *bona fide* transaction, because the claimant had no intention of pursuing any significant economic activity. The claimant had abused its rights by a '"*détournement de procédure*" consisting in the Claimant's creation of a legal fiction in order to gain access to an international arbitration procedure to which it was not entitled'.[35]

The uniform treatment of instances of fraud, misrepresentation, corruption or abuse of rights on the basis of the overriding principle of good faith and other principles derived from it shows the unifying role that a general principle of law may have in the reasoning of diverse arbitral tribunals. These four cases also show that tribunals have been undisturbed by doctrinal arguments on the meaning of general principles, and have applied them without entering into any discussion about their nature.

Reliance on principles, however, may not result in consistency and uniformity where multiple principles are at play. Views on which principle to apply, the opportunity of its application and its interpretation may vary from case to case. Tribunals may face the choice between opposite principles, where preference for one will result in detriment to the other, or they may diverge as to the placement of the scale pointer in seeking the right balance between them. The ideal outcome would be to fashion an overriding principle under which the apparently conflicting principles are subsumed and coordinated. This was the approach taken by the ICJ in

[31] *Phoenix Action Ltd* v. *Czech Republic*, ICSID Case No. ARB/06/5, Award, 15 April 2009, paras. 78–9, available at: http://icsid.worldbank.org/ICSID/.
[32] Ibid., para. 144. [33] Ibid., para. 109. [34] Ibid., para. 107.
[35] Ibid., para. 143. See also *Gustav F W Hamester GmbH & Co KG* v. *Republic of Ghana*, ICSID Case No. ARB/07/24, Award, 18 June 2010, paras. 123–4, available at: http://ita.law.uvic.ca/documents/Hamesterv.GhanaAward.pdf.

the *Gabčíkovo-Nagymaros* case, where the Court reconciled economic development and protection of the environment under the concept of sustainable development.[36] When this is not feasible, a choice in favour of one principle or another becomes inevitable, and the choice will normally depend on the policy preferences of the tribunal rather than on legal principle.[37]

The balance between the regulatory power of the State and the right to be compensated in cases of taking of property is an example of this. Tribunals have struggled between the criteria of the 'sole effects' and of the 'purpose' of the measures taken by the State to determine whether a compensable indirect expropriation has taken place. The abundant literature on the subject has, on the one hand, emphasized the difficulty that exists in determining where to draw the line and, on the other, it has noted that a clear line may never be drawn, given the need to balance public and private interests in each case. The assessment of the State's measures and their purpose on the basis of the principle of proportionality, a very common

[36] 'Throughout the ages, mankind has, for economic and other reasons constantly interfered with nature. In the past, this was often done without consideration of the effects upon the environment. Owing to new scientific insights and to a growing awareness of the risks for mankind – for present and future generations – of pursuit of such interventions at an unconsidered and unabated pace, new norms and standards have been developed, set forth in a great number of instruments during the last two decades. Such new norms have to be taken into consideration, and such new standards given proper weight, not only when States contemplate new activities but also when continuing with activities begun in the past. This need to reconcile economic development with protection of the environment is aptly expressed in the concept of sustainable development,' *Gabčíkovo-Nagymaros Project (Hungary/Slovakia)*, Judgment, ICJ Reports 1997, 7, 78 (para. 140). It is noteworthy that the Court referred to the concept and not the principle of sustainable development, but the reasoning of the Court is a good example of how to reconcile 'the new norms and standards' and past practices. V. Lowe argues that sustainable development is 'an interstitial principle, acting upon other, primary legal rules and principles – in this case, acting upon what the International Court took to be the legal principles of economic development and protection of the environment . . . ', 'The Politics of Law-Making: Are the Method and Character of Norm Creation Changing?' in M. Byers (ed.), *The Role of Law in International Politics* (Oxford University Press, 2000), 216.

[37] '[T]he choice is made by the judge not on the basis of the internal logic of the primary norms, but on the basis of extraneous factors. Those factors are many and varied. Two are obvious, and likely to carry great weight. The first is the consistency of the preferred outcome with what is thought, on broad moral and political grounds, to be "desirable" – a kind of broad equity. The second factor is the general cohesion of the preferred outcome with the existing norms of the legal system, which is in itself one of the desiderata of judicial decision-making. These factors are often, but not always, made explicit in the reasoning of the tribunal which is offered in justification of the decision', V. Lowe, 'The Politics of Law-Making'.

approach in human rights cases and used in the *Tecmed* decision,[38] has been held to be 'a helpful contribution to the evolution to the case law'.[39] In the determination of indirect expropriation, for instance, the principle of proportionality may serve to strike a balance between competing interests, much in the same way as the concept of sustainable development worked in the ICJ's decision in *Gabčíkovo-Nagymaros* to strike the balance between development and respect for the environment.

A further controversial issue is, when can a tribunal have recourse to general principles? The Tribunal in *SGS* v. *Pakistan* had recourse to the principle that 'a violation of a contract entered into by a State with an investor of another State, is not, by itself, a violation of international law' in determining the meaning of the umbrella clause in the investment treaty between Switzerland and Pakistan.[40] In turn, the Tribunal in *SGS* v. *Philippines* criticized the application of 'general principles of international law' to generate a presumption against the broad interpretation of the umbrella clause in the investment treaty between Switzerland and Pakistan and concluded that the question was 'essentially one of interpretation, and does not seem to be determined by any presumption'.[41]

And yet, recourse to principles or fundamental rules of international law may be used as a means of integrating a particular interpretation into international law. The Tribunal in *Maffezini* viewed the MFN clause as a means of harmonizing and enlarging the mechanisms of dispute settlement provided for in investment treaties and proceeded to integrate its interpretation of the clause within the general rules of international law.[42] Thus, it

[38] *Técnicas Medioambientales Tecmed, SA* v. *United Mexican States*, ICSID Case No. ARB(AF)/00/2, Award, 29 May 2003, 10 ICSID Reports 134, para. 122.

[39] L.Y. Fortier and S.L. Drymer, 'Indirect Expropriation in the Law of International Investment: I Know it When I See It, or *Caveat Investor*' *ICSID Review* 19 (2004) 326. See also U. Kriebaum, 'Privatizing Human Rights. The Interface Between International Investment Protection and Human Rights' 3(5) *TDM* (2006); C. Reiner and C. Schreuer, 'Human Rights and International Investment Arbitration', available at: www.univie.ac.at/intlaw/h_rights_int_invest_arbitr.pdf; and for the application of the principle of proportionality in other investment treaty cases, see Newcombe and Paradell, *Law Practice of Investment Treaties*, 363–6.

[40] *SGS Société Générale de Surveillance SA* v. *Islamic Republic of Pakistan*, ICSID Case No. ARB/01/13, Decision on Objections to Jurisdiction, 6 August 2003, 8 ICSID Reports 406, para. 167.

[41] *SGS Société Générale de Surveillance SA* v. *Republic of the Philippines*, ICSID Case No. ARB/02/6, Decision on Objections to Jurisdiction, 29 January 2004, 8 ICSID Reports 518, para. 122.

[42] *Maffezini* v. *Kingdom of Spain*, ICSID Case No. ARB/97/7, Decision on Objections to Jurisdiction, 25 January 2000, 5 ICSID Reports 396, para. 62.

held that if a party to a treaty had conditioned its consent to arbitration to the exhaustion of local remedies, this condition could not become inoperative by invoking the MFN clause 'in relation to a treaty with a third party which does not contain this element because the condition reflects a fundamental rule of international law'.[43] The balance between an interpretation that provides consistency of treatment through an MFN clause and the consistency of that interpretation with fundamental rules of international law has been more elusive in cases where tribunals have decided that the MFN clause may not be used to extend its reach to procedural matters, thus limiting the protection envisaged in the treaty to the substantive provisions.

[43] Ibid., para. 63.

7

Precedent

Even in a non-binding precedent system with multiple arbitral tribunals, precedents[1] may nonetheless create expectations for the future. The multiplicity of decisions has narrowed the discretion of tribunals, both in the case of their decision in following a previous award or their decision not to follow it. Even in the latter cases, previous decisions will provide a reference point for tribunals, which will need to distinguish their current cases from existing precedent.[2] Precedent exercises a 'latent control function' through 'the expectation that international tribunals will follow the law, whether its origin is statutory, customary or judicial'.[3] In a legal context, it is 'a manifestation of a deeply rooted human penchant for using analogical reasoning to make sense of, and to manage the complexity of the environment'.[4]

Precedent in arbitration in general, and particularly in investment treaty arbitration, has recently drawn substantial attention in view of the fact

1 Parts of this chapter in a somewhat different form were published in C. Binder *et al.* (eds.), *International Law for the 21st Century: Essays in Honor of Christoph Schreuer* (Oxford University Press, 2009), 830.

2 'The standards formulated in Article 3 of the Treaty, vague as they may be, are susceptible of specification through judicial practice and do in fact have sufficient legal content to allow the case to be decided on the basis of law. Over the last few years, a number of awards have dealt with such standards yielding a fair amount of practice that sheds light on their legal meaning', *Saluka Investments BV* v. *Czech Republic*, PCA, Partial Award, 17 March 2006, para. 284, available at www.pca-cpa.org/showpage.asp?pag_id=1149.

3 W.M. Reisman, 'The Supervisory Jurisdiction of the International Court of Justice: International Arbitration and International Adjudication' *Recueil des coursl* 258 (1996) 9, 32.

4 A.S. Sweet and M. McCrown, 'Discretion and Precedent in European Law', in O. Wiklund (ed.), *Judicial Discretion in European Perspective* (The Hague: Kluwer Law International, 2003), 99.

that most decisions and awards of arbitral tribunals are publicly available shortly after having been issued. In international law, as in English law, it may be said that 'the history of judicial precedent is intimately bound up with the history of the law reports'.[5] This heightened attention has also been prompted by the sometimes different or contradictory interpretations of the law adopted by international courts and tribunals, in view of their publicity and of the corresponding debates concerning the proliferation of courts and tribunals.

Jennings had already expressed his alarm and certain irritation when he asked about these tribunals: 'And what do they all do? And where do they sit? It is not easy to find out.' He then proceeded to comment:

> There is no kind of structured relationship between most of them. There is not even the semblance of any kind of hierarchy or system. They have appeared as need or desire or ambitions promoted yet another one. In this particular respect, contemporary international law is just a disorderly medley. Suffice it to say that it is very difficult to try to make any sort of pattern, much less a structured relationship, of this mass of tribunals, whether important or petty. It is sometimes difficult to find out what is going on, much less to study it.[6]

Buergenthal has been more positive about these developments. He understood the growth of international judicial and quasi-judicial dispute mechanisms as helping the transformation of international law into a

[5] T. Ellis Lewis, 'The History of Judicial Precedent' *LQR* 48 (1932) 230. See also T. Wälde, 'Confidential Awards as Precedent in Arbitration: Dynamics and Implication of Award Publication', in E. Gaillard and Y. Banifatemi (eds.), *The Precedent in International Arbitration* (Paris: IAI, 2008), 113.

[6] R.Y. Jennings, 'The Judiciary, International and National and the Development of International Law' *ICLQ* 45 (1996) 5. Judge Schwebel offers a different view: 'complete unity has never existed in international law; and its development has always been uneven. The body of international law has been able to absorb a measure of diversity in judicial and arbitral decisions. The processes of the incremental development of customary international law are neither uniform nor unified, treaty-making is bilateral as well as multilateral, and many multilateral treaties are not designed to attract, or do not attract, universal adherence. There is a measure of diversity among different regional traditions in international law, among competing political ideologies, and between the approaches of developed and less developed States of the international community. The divergence of view among international lawyers on questions of international law is obvious. This does not exclude the judges sitting on the Bench of the International Court of Justice', S. Schwebel, 'The Proliferation of International Tribunals: Threat or Promise?' in V. Lowe and M. Fitzmaurice (eds.), *Fifty Years of the International Court of Justice: Essays in Honour of Sir Robert Jennings* (Cambridge University Press, 2007), 3.

more vibrant and more relevant legal system than it has been in the past. This growth he attributed to a virtuous cycle: more cases produce more jurisprudence, more jurisprudence produces more cases which, in turn, increases the certainty of judicial outcomes.[7]

The States' desire for continuity and the assumed certainty and consistency in the decisions of a permanent court prompted the creation of the Permanent Court of International Justice, as opposed to the then recently created Permanent Court of Arbitration: 'There was no assurance that the decisions of the arbitrators chosen from the panel of the [Permanent] Court of Arbitration would serve a purpose other than of disposing of the dispute between the parties. They could not invariably be relied upon to develop and clarify international law.'[8] Shahabuddeen agreed with this, and in his Lauterpacht Lectures maintained that 'the very fact that the Court was established as a court of justice implied that its decisions would have some precedential effect'.[9]

However, permanence does not guarantee predictability. The permanence of the ICJ has to be weighed against the wider discretion that the Court has as compared to the discretion of arbitral tribunals. Rosenne has observed that 'The Court's interpretation of the integrity of its judicial function as established in the combined Charter and Statute gives it a wide measure of judicial discretion of whether and how it will deal with a case. An arbitral tribunal does not usually have such a wide measure of discretion. This can add an element of unpredictability.'[10]

Paradoxically, and notwithstanding the desire for continuity and consistency:

[7] T. Buergenthal, 'The Proliferation of Disputes, Dispute Settlement Procedures and Respect for the Rule of Law' *ICSID Rev.* 21 (2006) 126, 128.

[8] H. Lauterpacht, *Development of International Law by the International Court, being a revised edition of The Development of International Law by the Permanent Court of International Justice* (London: Stevens, 1958), 6. For Reisman, '[o]ne of the consequences of a standing tribunal is that its judgments are collected and become jurisprudence', Reisman, 'The Supervisory Jurisdiction of the International Court of Justice', 53.

[9] M. Shahabuddeen, *Precedent in the World Court* (Cambridge University Press, 1996), 159.

[10] He continued: 'there is a major difference between unpredictability based on counsel's understanding of what the law is, when each side knows the strengths and weaknesses of its own case and those of its opponent's, and unpredictability derived from fleeting and possibly subjective concepts of judicial discretion held by the majority of the day, and the general international political climate then prevailing', S. Rosenne, 'Some Thoughts on International Arbitration Today' *Israel Law Review* 27 (1993) 447.

> [S]overeign states are averse to any suggestion that compacts other than those to which they have consented may be invoked against them, so too are they unwilling to submit to the elaboration of international law by anything resembling the accretion of binding precedents known as common law.[11]

The tension between the desire of consistency and the State sovereignty found its way into Article 38 of the ICJ Statute, where judicial decisions were relegated to a subsidiary means of determination of the law subject to Article 59 of the Statute on *res judicata*. This notwithstanding, it is widely accepted that judicial pronouncements have an influence beyond the case and the parties concerned.[12] Indeed, Brierly has maintained that 'the influence of precedents in legal development is not wholly a matter of juridical theory or of the deliberate policy of judges. It has its source in the natural desire of any court to maintain consistency in the application of law'.[13] But there are also other reasons:

- the parties' expectation to be treated in accordance with the principle of equality before the law, which dictates that analogous situations be treated in analogous fashion and in accordance with objective considerations;[14]
- precedents are a repository of legal experience, since they embody what in the past has been considered as good law;
- to follow precedent is a way to avoid the appearance of any excess of judicial discretion; precedent imposes discipline upon the Tribunal's reasoning,[15] and a restraint on judges' use of personal reasons in deciding;[16]

[11] J. Paulsson, 'International Arbitration and the Generation of Legal Norms: Treaty Arbitration and International Law' *TDM* 3(5) (2006) 2.

[12] P. Weil, 'Cours général de droit international public' *Recueil* 237 (1992) 142. The Tribunal in *SGS* v. *Philippines* commented that Article 53(1) of the ICSID Convention, which provides that awards are 'binding on the parties', 'might be regarded as directed to the *res judicata* effect of awards rather than their impact as precedents in later cases', see *SGS Société Générale de Surveillance SA* v. *Republic of the Philippines*, ICSID Case No. ARB/02/6, Decision on Objections to Jurisdiction, 29 January 2004, 8 ICSID Reports 518, para. 97.

[13] J.L. Brierly, 'The Basis of Obligation in International Law', in H. Lauterpacht and C.H.M. Waldock (eds.), *The Basis of Obligation in International Law and Other Papers by the Late James Leslie Brierly* (Oxford: Clarendon Press, 1958), 29.

[14] Weil, 'Cours général de droit international public', 141.

[15] *Glamis Gold, Ltd.* v. *The United States of America*, UNCITRAL Award, 8 June 2009, 5 (para. 7), available at: www.state.gov/documents/organization/125798.pdf.

[16] R. Posner, *How Judges Think* (Cambridge, Mass.: Harvard University Press, 2008), 145.

- judges are reluctant to admit that they were wrong;[17] and
- judges are strongly motivated to adhere to precedent in order to encourage adherence to the precedents they create and to limit their workloads.[18]

There are also specific reasons to follow precedent that are proper to the state of development of international law. Due to the lack of legislative action with binding effect, 'judicial pronouncements of one kind or another constitute the principal method by which the law can find some concrete measure of clarification and development'.[19] International custom and general principles of law have been described as woolly categories 'inherently unlikely to produce specific answers to precise questions. For this, lawyers naturally search for *precedents.*'[20]

While these reasons explain why precedents are followed or are particularly significant in international law, they also point to the difficulties that international tribunals may face in establishing a *jurisprudence constante*: first, there is the indeterminacy inherent in the graphic description of 'woolly categories'. Second, even when it comes to treaty interpretation, as we have seen in the preceding chapters, the terms may be so general that in applying them to the specific situation a certain degree of subjectivity cannot be excluded.[21] Third, in the words of Crawford, 'some of the devices which the International Court has available to it which conduce to at least some

[17] Lauterpacht, *Development of International Law*, 14. [18] Posner, *How Judges Think*, 145.

[19] Separate Opinion of Judge Fitzmaurice, *Barcelona Traction Light and Power Company, Limited*, Judgment, ICJ Reports 1970, 64, 64 (para. 2). The doctrine has focused on the lack of a central legislative authority and the mainly customary nature of international law. Virally stated that: 'A judicial or arbitral decision . . . represents an opinion as to the actual content of international law . . . It has further a special value in a system of law which is in great part customary and is to be ascertained in consequence through considerable research into precedents', P Virally, 'The Sources of International Law', in M. Sørensen (ed.), *Manual of Public International Law* (London: Macmillan, 1968), 150. Weil has noted that: '[e]n l'absence d'un pouvoir législatif, c'est en effet le juge qui, le plus souvent, vient combler les interstices de la normativité internationale', Weil, 'Cours général de droit international public', 142. On interstitial norms as engines of change in international law, see V. Lowe, 'Politics of Law-Making and Character of Norm Creation Changing?' in M. Byers (ed.), *The Role of Law in International Politics* (Oxford University Press, 2000), 207–26.

[20] Paulsson, ' International Arbitration', 1–2.

[21] C. de Visscher, *Problèmes d'interpretation judiciaire en droit international public* (Paris: Pédone, 1963), 46. This subjectivity finds expression in looking for 'the thread that will guide us to the correct solution in the midst of sometimes contradictory practices and ambiguous or too general texts', ibid., 13.

consistency in its jurisprudence do not exist' in investment treaty arbitration.[22] Article 63 of the ICJ Statute concerning intervention in proceedings before the Court is a good example of one such device.

This situation contrasts with the purpose of investment treaties. These treaties are part of a wider trend aimed at fostering predictability in specific legal environments. Indeed, arbitral tribunals themselves have found that legal stability and respect for the expectations of investors are part of the treatment guaranteed by the treaties. It would be consistent with such findings that arbitral tribunals consider that their decisions and awards are part of the treatment and expectations guaranteed by the treaty and, in consequence, that stability and consistency form part of their function. Bearing this in mind, how have tribunals fared?

To answer this question, I will first review how arbitral tribunals have weighed the importance of precedent and then discuss the role of values in shaping precedents and precedent interpretation.

1. The weight of precedent

As a first step, arbitral tribunals consistently acknowledge that in international law there is no doctrine of binding precedent, and that they are not bound by precedents. For instance, in *LESI and Astaldi*, where the Tribunal was composed of the same members as the Tribunal in *Consortium LESI-DIPENTA*, the parties had accepted that the documentation used in these earlier proceedings was an integral part of the later case. This notwithstanding, the Tribunal considered it necessary to affirm that 'these proceedings are formally independent from the first and that decision and reasoning developed there do not benefit of the authority of *res judicata*'.[23] The Tribunal then warned that, although the members of the current Tribunal were the same as those of the first Tribunal, they were not obliged to follow the positions taken in respect of the respondent's objections to the jurisdiction of the Tribunal or of the admissibility of the arbitration request, even when their terms were sometimes identical.

To prove their distance from precedent and their independent reasoning, some tribunals first reach their decision and then address the precedents

[22] J. Crawford, 'Similarity of Issues in Disputes Arising under the Same or Similarly Drafted Investment Treaties', in Gaillard and Banifatemi (eds.), *The Precedent in International Arbitration*, 98.

[23] *LESI, SpA and Astaldi, SpA* v. *People's Democratic Republic of Algeria*, ICSID Case No. ARB/05/3, Decision on Jurisdiction, 12 July 2006, para. 56, available at: http://icsid.worldbank.org/ICSID/ (translated by the author).

adduced by the parties. For example, the *Gas Natural* Tribunal, after reaching its decision, emphasized that it had reached it independently, without considering itself bound by any other judgments or arbitral awards. However, the Tribunal thought it *useful* to compare its conclusion with the conclusions reached in other recent ICSID arbitrations. After the comparison, the Tribunal said that it was 'satisfied that its analyses and decisions, independently arrived at, are consistent with the conclusions of other arbitral tribunals faced with similar issues'.[24]

The care of arbitral tribunals to express their independence is understandable. In the case of ICSID tribunals, Schreuer and Weineger have warned against the possibility of 'an application for annulment that alleges an excess of powers or a failure to state reasons because the tribunal has simply relied on earlier decisions without making an independent decision or developing its own reasons'.[25]

Notwithstanding expressions of independence of reasoning and decision making, tribunals may take the initiative and invite the parties to comment on precedents which may have been published at a stage of the proceedings too late for the parties to have brought them up, or they may refer to decisions considered to be relevant for the decision irrespective of the timing of their publication. The *Malaysian Historical Salvors* case is a good example of this. The sole arbitrator took the initiative to request in three instances the comments of the parties on cases not adduced by them.[26]

[24] *Gas Natural SDG, SA* v. *Argentine Republic*, ICSID Case No. ARB/03/10, Decision on Preliminary Questions on Jurisdiction, 17 June 2005, 14 ICSID Reports 284, para. 52. Tribunals also deny that their own decisions or awards would serve as a precedent. For instance, on that ground the Tribunal in *Methanex* dismissed the argument of Mexico that acceptance of *amicus curiae* briefs would constitute a precedent. In the words of the Tribunal: 'This tribunal can set no legal precedent, in general or at all. It has no power for other arbitration tribunals how to interpret Article 15(1); and in a later arbitration, there may be other circumstances leading the tribunal to exercise its discretion differently. For each arbitration, the decision must be made by its tribunal in the particular circumstances of that arbitration only', *Methanex* v. *United States*, UNCITRAL (NAFTA), Decision on Petitions from Third Persons to Intervene as 'Amici Curiae', 15 January 2001, 7 ICSID Reports 224, para. 51.

[25] C. Schreuer and M. Weiniger, 'Conversations across Cases – Is there a Doctrine of Precedent in Investment Arbitration?' *TDM* 5(3) (2008) 8.

[26] *Malaysian Historical Salvors, SDN, BHD* v. *Malaysia*, ICSID Case No. ARB/05/10, Decision on Jurisdiction, 17 May 2007, paras. 49–52, available at: http://icsid.worldbank.org/ICSID/. The sole arbitrator first requested comments on the Decisions on Jurisdiction in the cases of *Bayindir Insaat Turizm Ticaret Ve Sanayi AS* v. *Islamic Republic of Pakistan*, ICSID Case No. ARB/03/29, Decision on Jurisdiction, 14 November 2005, available at: http://icsid.worldbank.org/ICSID/, and *Československa obchodní banka (CSOB), as* v. *Slovak Republic*, ICSID Case No. ARB/97/4, Decision on Objections to Jurisdiction,

Similarly, in *Zhinvali* the Tribunal heard the parties' views on the *Mihaly* award. The Tribunal became aware of this award before the filing of post-hearing briefs. The president of the Tribunal brought it to the attention of the parties and their counsel and post-hearing reply pleadings were postponed so that the parties could take the award into account in their submissions.[27] Eventually the *Mihaly* award played a significant role in the reasoning of the Tribunal in *Zhinvali*. However, it is difficult for an external observer to assess the extent to which tribunals take the initiative and invite the parties to comment on awards which they may have overlooked. This is partly so in view of the impossibility of ascertaining whether a particular tribunal was itself aware of recent or other awards when the parties have not cited them.

Other tribunals have, instead, refused to take into account late submissions of cases by the parties. Indeed, tribunals are often concerned about the need to conduct the proceedings in an efficient manner and late submission of cases by the parties, whether at their own initiative or at the Tribunal's prompting, may lengthen the proceedings. This consideration, for instance, weighed on the initial decision of the *Sempra* Tribunal not to consider the award in the case of *LG&E* introduced by the respondent at a late stage of the proceedings. That Tribunal justified the refusal as follows:

> The Tribunal is mindful of the parties' wish and right to fully present their cases. The Tribunal also understands its duty to conduct the proceedings in an orderly and efficient manner. The Tribunal is confident that the parties in these proceedings have been given plenty of opportunities to fully present their arguments on each issue in dispute. Accepting Argentina's non-invited submission at this late stage of the proceedings would open the door for a never ending exchange of arguments, unduly burdening both parties.[28]

But once precedents are before a Tribunal, whether by initiative of the parties or of its own, what weight must the Tribunal attribute to them?

24 May 1999, 5 ICSID Reports 335. A week later, the arbitrator requested comments on the recently issued Decision of the Annulment Committee in the case of *Patrick Mitchell* v. *Democratic Republic of the Congo*, ICSID Case No. ARB/99/7, Annulment, 1 November 2006, available at: http://ita.law.uvic.ca/documents/mitchellannulment.pdf, and about four months later he requested comments on the Decision on Jurisdiction in *PSEG Global Inc. and Konya Ilgin Elektrik Üretim ve Ticaret Limited Sirketi* v. *Republic of Turkey*, ICSID Case No. ARB/02/5, Decision on Jurisdiction, 4 June 2004, 11 ICSID Reports 434.

[27] *Zhinvali Development Ltd* v. *Republic of Georgia*, ICSID Case No. ARB/00/1, Award, 24 January 2003, 10 ICSID Reports 6, 86–7.

[28] *Sempra Energy International* v. *The Argentine Republic*, ICSID Case No. ARB/02/16, Decision of 28 February 2007, quoted in the Award, 28 September 2007, para. 53, available at: http://icsid.worldbank.org/ICSID/.

Referring to precedents adduced by the parties, Fitzmaurice commented that, in such cases, the precedent is cited 'as something *which the tribunal cannot ignore*, which it is bound to take into consideration and (by implication) which it ought to follow unless the decision can be shown to have been clearly wrong, or distinguishable from the extant, or in some way legally or factually inapplicable'.[29] Even more so would be the case of the precedents on which the Tribunal had taken the initiative to invite the parties to file observations.

A review of awards shows that the practice of tribunals varies and that it could be classified in four categories, depending on the weight attributed to precedent in their reasoning.

(a) In the first, which could be denominated the 'persuasive' category, tribunals have:

- found it to be 'a reasonable assumption that international arbitral tribunals, including those set up within ICSID, will generally take into account the precedents set by other international tribunals';[30]
- found the interpretations of other tribunals to be instructive;[31]
- stated that they would certainly carefully consider other tribunals' decisions whenever appropriate;[32]
- noted that their task was rendered easier by the fact that a number of recent cases had to discuss and decide on similar or comparable provisions concerning contracts and the scope of a particular treaty;[33]
- found that precedents may be considered as a matter of inspiration;[34] or
- analysed precedents 'to discern a broad trend which emerges from ICSID jurisprudence'.[35]

[29] G. Fitzmaurice, 'Some Problems Regarding the Formal Sources of International Law', in *Symbolae Verzijl: Présentées au professeur J. H. W. Verzijl à l'occasion de son LXXX-ième anniversaire* (The Hague: Martinus Nijhoff, 1958) 153, 172, quoted in Jennings, 'The Judiciary, International and National and the Development of International Law', 9 (emphasis in original).

[30] *BP American Production Co* v. *Argentine Republic*, ICSID Case No. ARB/04/8, Decision on Jurisdiction, 27 July 2006, para. 42, available at: http://icsid.worldbank.org/ICSID/.

[31] *Liberian Eastern Timber Corporation (LETCO)* v. *The Republic of Liberia*, ICSID Case No. ARB/83/2, Award, 31 March 1986, 2 ICSID Reports 346, 352.

[32] *Jan de Nul NV and Dredging International NV* v. *Arab Republic of Egypt*, ICSID Case No. ARB/04/13, Decision on Jurisdiction, 16 June 2006, para. 131, available at: http://ita.law.uvic.ca/documents/JandeNuljurisdiction061606.pdf.

[33] *CMS Gas Transmission Company* v. *Argentine Republic*, ICSID Case No. ARB/01/8, Award, 12 May 2005, 14 ICSID Reports 158, para. 72.

[34] *AES Corporation* v. *The Argentine Republic*, ICSID Case No. ARB/02/17, Decision on Jurisdiction, 26 April 2005, 12 ICSID Reports 312, para. 31.

[35] *Malaysian Historical Salvors*, para. 104.

(b) The second category includes awards or decisions where tribunals have distinguished the instant case from preceding cases that may be considered relevant but that, for the reasons stated by the Tribunal, are not. This approach seems to express a higher concern for consistency, since it requires a more proactive attention to precedent by the Tribunal. For instance, the *Aucoven* Tribunal referred to the different conclusion reached by the Tribunal in *Banro* in a similar case and justified what could appear as a departure from that decision on the basis of the different circumstances of the case at hand.[36]

In *Sempra* the respondent requested the disqualification of all three members of the Tribunal after their refusal to admit the *LG&E* award. Before the request was denied, the Secretary-General of ICSID wrote to the members of the Tribunal 'requesting them to confirm her understanding that the Tribunal, like other ICSID tribunals, gives due consideration to published decisions, in particular, the Decision of Liability issued in ICSID Case No. ARB/02/01 (*LG&E Energy Corp., LG&E Capital Corp. and LG&E International Inc v Argentine Republic*)'.[37] The *Sempra* Tribunal responded:

> The Tribunal has examined with particular attention the recent decision on liability and subsequent award on damages in the *LG&E* case as they have dealt with mostly identical questions concerning emergency and state of necessity. The decision on liability has been contrasted with the finding of the Tribunal in *CMS*. While two arbitrators sitting in the present case were also members of the tribunal in the *CMS* case the matter has been examined anew. This Tribunal must note, first, that in addition to differences in the legal interpretation of the Treaty in this context, an important question that distinguishes the *LG&E* decision on liability from *CMS*, and for that matter also from the recent award in *Enron*, lies in the assessment of the facts.[38]

Despite the initial refusal to take it into account, in the end the Tribunal examined the decision in question and justified the different course it took by distinguishing it on the basis of its own appreciation of the facts and a different understanding of the treaty of reference.

At times a tribunal may dismiss precedents with a wave of the hand for not being convincing or to the point:

[36] *Autopista Concesionada de Venezuela (Aucoven), CA* v. *Bolivarian Republic of Venezuela*, ICSID Case No. ARB/00/5, Decision on Jurisdiction, 27 September 2001, 6 ICSID Reports 419, para. 143.

[37] *Sempra*, para. 63. This was an unprecedented step predicated by the circumstances rather than by an institutional pursuit of consistent case law.

[38] Ibid., para. 346.

They [awards dealing with the MFN jurisdictional implications] are of uneven persuasiveness and relevance. The present Tribunal would find it jejune to declare that there is a dominant view; it is futile to make a head-count of populations of such diversity. What can be said with confidence is that a *jurisprudence constante* of general applicability is not yet firmly established.[39]

(c) The third category includes decisions where precedent was used to reinforce interpretations made in accordance with Article 32 of the Vienna Convention on the Law of Treaties. This is the case in *Canadian Cattlemen*, where the Tribunal reinforced the relevance of precedent by linking Article 32 of the Vienna Convention on the Law of Treaties with the provisions of Article 38 of the Statute of the ICJ. In the words of the Tribunal, this article:

permits, as supplementary means of interpretation, not only *preparatory work* and *circumstances of conclusion* of the treaty, but indicates by the word "including" that, beyond these two means expressly mentioned, other supplementary means may be applied. Article 38 [para. 1.d] of the Statute of the International Court of Justice provides that judicial decisions are applicable for the interpretation of public international law as "subsidiary means". Therefore, they must be understood to be also *supplementary means of interpretation* in the sense of Article 32 VCLT.[40]

The Tribunal then considered carefully the various cases produced by the parties and weighed their relative merits in support of its own conclusions, but, in accordance with Article 32, it limited their relevance to decisions of other tribunals which confirmed the meaning resulting from the application of Article 31.

(d) The fourth category includes decisions in which tribunals have referred to a 'duty to adopt solutions established in a series of consistent cases'. The *Saipem* case is a good example. In that case, the Tribunal believed that:

subject to compelling contrary grounds, it has a duty to adopt solutions established in a series of consistent cases. It also believes that, subject to the specifics of a given treaty and of the circumstances of the actual case, it has a duty to seek to contribute to the harmonious development of investment law and thereby to

[39] *Renta 4 SVSA et al* v. *Russian Federation*, SCC No. 24/2007, Award on Preliminary Objections, 20 March 2009, para. 94, available at: http://ita.law.uvic.ca/documents/Renta.pdf.

[40] *Canadian Cattlemen for Fair Trade* v. *United States*, UNCITRAL (NAFTA), Award on Jurisdiction, 28 January 2008, para. 50, available at: http://ita.law.uvic.ca/documents/CCFT-USAAward_001.pdf.

meet the legitimate expectations of the community of States and investors towards certainty of the rule of law.[41]

This was the first time that an arbitral tribunal had spoken of a *duty* to adopt solutions adopted in a series of consistent cases and of the *duty* to contribute to the harmonious development of investment law. The same concern for systemic coherence was expressed by the *Glamis* Tribunal:

The reality is that Chapter 11 of the NAFTA contains a significant public system of private investment protection. The ultimate integrity of the protections given to the many individual investments made under Chapter 11 is ensured by reference to a multitude of arbitral panels occupied by persons who are only occasionally reappointed. The ultimate integrity of the Chapter 11 system as a whole requires a modicum of awareness of each of these tribunals for each other and the system as a whole.

The fact that any particular tribunal need not live with the challenge of applying its reasoning in the case before it to a host of different future disputes (the challenge faced by standing adjudicative bodies) does not mean such a tribunal can ignore that challenge. A case-specific mandate is not a license to ignore systemic implications. To the contrary, it arguably makes it all the more important that each tribunal renders its case-specific decision with sensitivity to the position of future tribunals and an awareness of other systemic implications.[42]

Having reviewed how tribunals deal with precedent, a further question to be examined is the extent to which arbitral tribunals view their own awards as setting future precedents. For instance, in *Methanex* Mexico argued against the admissibility of *amicus curiae* on the basis that the decision to accept would serve as a precedent. The *Methanex* Tribunal dismissed the argument:

This tribunal can set no legal precedent, in general or at all. It has no power for other arbitration tribunals how to interpret Article 15(1); and in a later arbitration, there may be other circumstances leading the tribunal to exercise its discretion differently. For each arbitration, the decision must be made by its tribunal in the particular circumstances of that arbitration only.[43]

[41] *Saipem SpA* v. *People's Republic of Bangladesh*, ICSID Case No. ARB/05/7, Decision on Jurisdiction, 21 March 2007, (2007) 22 *ICSID Rev – FILJ* 100, para. 57. This duty of the international judge was recognized long ago by Sir Hersch Lauterpacht: '[The international judge is] bound to adduce reasons for departing from the obligation of consistency and of observance of settled principles', in *Development of International Law*, 15.

[42] *Glamis*, 2 (paras. 5–6).

[43] *Methanex*, para. 51. Cf. the opinion of K. Highet, 'The precedential significance of this Award for future proceedings under the North American Free Trade Agreement (NAFTA) cannot be underestimated. In addition, the Award will be an important

The formalism of the Tribunal is surprising, since it sought precedents to support its own decision.[44]

In the case of *RosInvest*, a member of the Tribunal was sufficiently concerned that the Tribunal's interpretation of the MFN clause might influence future tribunals to insert his individual declaration within the text of the decision:

I would not want our common conclusion that Article 8 does not confer jurisdiction in this case to be taken in any way as an expression of opinion on how that article or other similar treaty clauses relate to other claims that might be brought forward in other cases based on an allegation of expropriation.[45]

The issue of whether the weight of an arbitral award is diminished by a majority vote as opposed to a unanimous decision deserves separate treatment. It is assumed that a unanimous decision of a multi-member tribunal reflects a compromise,[46] and this tendency to compromise has been decried.[47] But, while compromise may be necessary in a large

guidance to future potential NAFTA claimants. It is for this purpose that as complete an understanding as possible be expressed of the legal issues involved', Dissenting Opinion, Introductory paragraph, *Waste Management, Inc.* v. *Mexico*, ICSID Case No. ARB(AF)/98/2 (NAFTA, Award on Jurisdiction, available at: http://ita.law.uvic.ca/documents/WasteMgmt-Jurisdiction-dissent.pdf).

44 On *amici curiae* briefs, Fuller has noted that when certain groups have a long interest in the development of the law and are heard by a tribunal, a judicial proceeding turns more into a legislative hearing: 'The analogy to such a hearing becomes even stronger when the brief *amicus curiae* is employed, L.L. Fuller, *Anatomy of the Law* (Harmondsworth: Penguin Books, 1968), 147.

45 *RosInvestCo UK Ltd* v. *The Russian Federation*, SCC Case No. Arb V079/2005, Award on Jurisdiction, October 2007, para. 123, available at: http://ita.law.uvic.ca/documents/RosInvestjurisdiction_decision_2007_10_001.pdf. This statement is used by the *Renta* Tribunal to distinguish it from *RosInvest* without any consideration related to the fact that it was an individual statement, not a view of the Tribunal, see *Renta*, para. 48.

46 Reisman, 'The Supervisory Jurisdiction of the International Court of Justice', 294–5.

47 'The current trend is towards consensus and compromise, in dispute settlement as well as in the creation of international obligations. Some disapprove of the practice of delivering multiple judgments – majority, separate, dissenting – in the course of the decision of a single case. But international law would be impoverished without them. To force a tribunal which lacks compulsory jurisdiction and which has more than one member to render a single judgment is to force the tribunal down the path of compromise. Desirable as compromise might be in circumstances where the concern of dispute settlement procedure is to find a *modus vivendi* for the future – as in [*sic.*] the case in the WTO disputes procedures, for example – it is less obviously desirable where the parties to litigation have entered into a legal relationship on the basis of a deliberate acceptance of specific rights and duties. In such cases, there is still much to be said for an approach that upholds the rights and duties possessed by the Parties', V. Lowe, 'Shareholders' Rights to Control and Manage: From *Barcelona Traction* to *ELSI*' in N. Ando, E. McWhinney and

tribunal like the ICJ, it may not be presumed in a three-member panel. Arbitrators may agree with the decision for many reasons: they could genuinely agree with the decision, or they may decide to go along with it out of a sense of collegiality,[48] or just to provide the required majority. Posner maintained that '[a] judge might join the majority opinion in a case not because he agreed with it but because he thought that dissenting publicly would magnify the effect of the majority opinion by drawing attention to it'.[49] Sometimes members of tribunals are candid and explain their favourable vote notwithstanding their disagreement with the decision.[50] In other instances, however, the disagreement among members of the tribunal remains undisclosed, and in these circumstances the reasons of the favourable vote of a particular member to an award can only be surmised by the support of contradictory decisions by the same arbitrator.[51]

R. Wolfrum (eds.), *Liber Amicorum Judge Shigeru Oda* (The Hague: Kluwer Law International, 2002), 283–4. In the same vein, see Gros, 'La recherche du consensus dans les décisions de la Cour Internationale de Justice' in Rudolf Bernhardt (ed.), *Völkerrecht als Rechtsordnung, internationale Gerichtsbarkeit, Menschenrechte: Festschrift für Hermann Mosler* (Berlin: Springer, 1983), 358.

48 Scheneiderman uses, among others, the case of A.J. van den Berg in support of his argument that arbitrators are strategic in their decisions. He refers to van den Berg's statement to the parties, as reported in the *Investment Treaties News* issue of 1 April 2008 that 'he takes the view that collegiality demands that arbitrators sitting on three-member tribunals reach a common view as to how the case should be resolved', see D. Scheneiderman, 'Judicial Politics and International Investment Arbitration: Seeking an Explanation for Conflicting Outcomes', available at: http://works.bepress.com/david_schneiderman/1. Posner has observed in respect of appellate judges that: 'Dissent aversion reflects the simultaneous difficulty and importance of collegiality. Appellate judging is a cooperative enterprise. It does not work well when the judges' relations with one another become tinged with animosity – and that is always a danger because of the way in which the members of the cooperative enterprise are selected. Judges neither choose their colleagues and successors, as members of law firms and academic faculties do, nor are chosen . . . by a stable, uniform management layer above them.' Posner, *How Judges Think*, 33. A similar observation could be made in respect of arbitrators. See also the distinction between larger and smaller courts where collegiality is more important, 110–11.

49 Ibid., 10.

50 As in the case of van den Berg quoted above, or the examples of the Iran-US Claims Tribunal pointed out by S. Schwebel, 'The Majority Vote of an International Arbitral Tribunal' in *Justice in International Law: Selected Writings of Stephen M. Schwebel* (Cambridge University Press, 2008), 213–22.

51 Deliberation may change the views of an arbitrator or a judge because '[f]or a ruling to be an act of judgment rather than of will, a judge must be open to new ideas and willing to subject her own views to careful scrutiny', D.A. Farber and S. Sherry, *Judgment Calls* (Oxford University Press, 2009), 91.

While multiple opinions make possible the bold and innovative handling of cases by judges,[52] even assisting interpreters better to grasp the position of a tribunal, in the current status of the law it may not be such a negative behaviour to search for compromise, as the ICJ maintained.[53] Usually those who decry compromise assume a non-existent certainty of rights and obligations. In medieval England, a tribunal would not decide until it had reached a compromise which permitted a unanimous decision.[54] Indeed, compromise better suits the primary function of tribunals to settle the dispute at hand, even on the narrowest of grounds. This is all the more so in the case of *ad hoc* tribunals.

To conclude: first, from a systemic point of view, arbitral tribunals in investment cases have made ample use of judicial and quasi-judicial decisions in other jurisdictions. Outside of the ambit of investment treaty arbitration, references to ICJ case law are the most frequent, but we also find references to decisions of the European Court of Human Rights, the WTO Appeal Mechanism, the Iran-US Claims Tribunal, the Inter-American Court of Human Rights, etc. Sometimes reference is also made to decisions of national courts in support of a point made by the tribunal,[55] or

[52] V. Lowe, 'Shareholders' Rights to Control and Manage: From *Barcelona Traction* to *ELSI*', 284.

[53] *Application for Review of Judgment No. 333 of the United Nations Administrative Tribunal*, Advisory Opinion, ICJ Reports (1987) 18, 45–6 (paras. 49–50).

[54] 'The trial judge is now regarded as a "court of first instance", and a review of his decision by a panel of judges must therefore be by way of appeal. Under the *nisi prius* system, however, the trial judge was not a court capable of giving judgment; his task ended when the verdict was given, and the verdict was then returned to the full court of three or four judges so that they could give judgment. The kind of attention now given to cases on appeal could therefore be given, under the old system, before judgment was entered. It followed that when judgment was given in banc it should be regarded as final and conclusive. Indeed, the finality of a recorded judgment accounts for the reluctance of the medieval judges to enter a judgment at all if a division of opinion occurred on the bench. In case of doubt, proceedings would be adjourned as often as necessary to enable the doubts to be fully explored and for the judges to deliver their 'arguments' (in effect tentative judgments), which could be reviewed on successive occasions until a consensus of judicial opinion was found. Delays which might now seem intolerable were regarded as acceptable, indeed as essential to the deliberative process. The present system has sacrificed some of this circumspection to the avoidance of delay, but insures against error by providing for an appeal after judgment', see J.H. Baker, *An Introduction to English Legal History* (4th edn, London: Butterworths, 2002), 135–6.

[55] See, for instance, *Maffezini* v. *Kingdom of Spain*, ICSID Case No. ARB/97/7, Decision on Objections to Jurisdiction, 25 January 2000, 5 ICSID Reports 396, footnote 22 to para. 54; *Gustav F W Hamester GmbH & Co KG* v. *Republic of Ghana*, ICSID Case No. ARB/07/24, Award, 18 June 2010, para. 194, available at: http://ita.law.uvic.ca/documents/Hamesterv.GhanaAward.pdf.

simply to show that certain reasoning of an arbitral tribunal had been followed in a national court.[56]

Second, while reliance on case law may expand as the decided cases increase,[57] so have the constructive possibilities of analogy[58] and the opportunities of contradiction. Research on the weight of precedents in a common law jurisdiction shows that their influence evolves over time:

While we cannot draw any firm conclusions from these initial results, they suggest that the influence and precedent may change over time . . . In the initial period, attitudes clearly impact judicial decision making because judges must create legal doctrine almost from whole cloth . . . Following the development of some clear precedents, however, the influence of attitudes may be moderated as judges feel bound by those clear and controlling decisions. As more time passes and more precedents are decided, however, the proliferation of available prior decisions in turn expands judges' discretion to decide cases in accordance with their attitudes simply because they have more precedents from which to choose.[59]

Third, in reaching their decisions tribunals are not always guided by the impact that their award will have in the development of the law, either because they take the formal view of the non-binding character of precedent in international law or do not share the values underlying the extant awards and show a higher regard for following their own values than the certainty that would result by following precedent.

2. Precedent and values

As noted at the beginning of the chapter, precedents have been the subject of attention because of the need for consistency for the development of

[56] The Tribunal in *Renta* recalled that the English Court of Appeal had cited with approval in *Ecuador* v. *Occidental* the following statement made in *SGS* v. *Philippines*, para. 116: 'The BIT is a treaty for the promotion and reciprocal protection of investments. According to the preamble it is intended "to create and maintain favorable conditions for investments by investors of one Contracting Party in the territory of the other". It is legitimate to resolve uncertainties in its interpretation so as to favor the protection of covered investments', *Renta*, para. 57. For the judgment of the Court of Appeal in *Occidental* v. *Ecuador*, see *Ecuador* v. *Occidental Exploration & Production Co*, Court of Appeal – Commercial Court, 2 March 2006, [2006] EWHC 345 (Comm).

[57] J.P. Commission, 'Precedent in Investment Treaty Arbitration' *Journal of International Arbitration* 24 (2007) 129, 150–1.

[58] de Visscher, 44.

[59] S. Lindquist and F. Cross 'Empirically Testing Dworkin's Chain Novel Theory' *New York University Law Review* 80 (2005) 1156, 1204. See also comments by Posner, according to whom 'the landscape of case law is littered with inconsistent precedents among which

a *jurisprudence constante*. Consistency is determined not only by the weight that precedents may be given, but also by the values or policies that they reflect.[60] When tribunals are called to interpret texts which are silent on a particular matter, interpretation normally relies on an order of values.[61] The influence of values in the development of a *jurisprudence constante* can be evidenced in the manner in which a variety of adjudicatory bodies have dealt with the issue of whether they have the power to receive *amicus curiae* submissions.

When the Appellate Body of the World Trade Organization (WTO) was confronted with this issue, it decided that authority to receive *amicus curiae* briefs was part of its general power to draw working procedures under Article 17.9 of the Dispute Settlement Understanding.[62] The *Methanex* Tribunal, a NAFTA Tribunal established under UNCITRAL Arbitration Rules, reached a similar conclusion under Article 15(1), which grants discretion to the arbitral tribunal to 'conduct the arbitration in such manner as it considers appropriate, provided that the parties are treated with equality and that at any stage of the proceedings each party is given a full opportunity of presenting his case'. After finding that this provision was sufficient to justify its conclusion, it noted that its approach was supported by the practice of the Iran-US Claims Tribunal and WTO.[63] In particular, the *Methanex* Tribunal considered the Iran-US Claims Tribunal's interpretive notes on Article 15(1) of the UNCITRAL Arbitration Rules – agreed on by both Iran and the United States – which allow 'under special circumstances, any other person' than the parties 'to assist the arbitral tribunal

current judges can pick and choose, resurrecting if need be a precedent that had died but had not been given a decent burial', 45.

60 'The original precedent in a line of precedents could not have been based on precedent. At the origin of the line must be something else. It might well be a policy judgment or, what often will amount to the same thing, the interpretation of a vague statute or vague constitutional provision – and the policy judgment or the policy-laden interpretation might well be determined by ideology', ibid., 44.

61 de Visscher, *Problèmes d'interprétation*, 14.

62 See *Asbestos* litigation, *European Communities – Measures affecting asbestos and products containing asbestos*, WT/DS135/AB/R, 5 April 2001, paras. 52–5, where the Appellate Body publicly invited briefs from all interested sources, a power that it based on article 16.1 of the Working Procedures for Appellate Review; *Lead and Bismuth II*, *United States – Imposition of Countervailing Duties on Certain Hot-Rolled Lead and Bismuth Carbon Steel Products Originating in the United Kingdom*, WT/DS138/AB/R, 7 June 2000, para. 43, where the Appellate Body considered that it had the right to consider *amici curiae* briefs on the basis of its broad authority to adopt procedural rules established in article 17(9) of the DSU (provided they do not contradict the DSU or covered agreements).

63 *Methanex*, paras. 32–3.

by presenting written [or] oral statements'.[64] The *Methanex* Tribunal found that:

the authoritative guide to the exercise of the Iran-US Claim Tribunal's discretion under Article 15(1) and this award [Award No. 63-A/15-FT] demonstrate that the receipt of written submissions from a non-party third person does not necessarily offend the philosophy of international arbitration involving cases and non-state parties.[65]

The *Methanex* Tribunal also compared the procedural power of the WTO under Article 17.9 of the Dispute Settlement Understanding with that of the Tribunal under Article 15(1) of UNCITRAL, and observed that the power under Article 17.9 was 'significantly less broad'.[66] This led the *Methanex* Tribunal to conclude that:

for present purposes, this WTO practice demonstrates that the scope of a procedural power can extend to the receipt of written submissions from no-party third persons, even in a juridical procedure affecting the rights and obligations of state parties, and further it also demonstrates that the receipt of such submissions confers no rights, procedural or substantive, on such persons.[67]

When in the case of *Aguas Argentinas and others* v. *Argentina* an ICSID Tribunal was faced with the question whether it had the power to allow *amicus curiae* submissions, it could draw on the experience of the Iran-US Claims Tribunal, WTO and the NAFTA cases administered by ICSID. By then, the NAFTA Free Trade Commission had issued its Statement on Non-Disputing Party Participation and the ICSID Tribunal had no difficulty in reaching the conclusion that the acceptance of *amicus curiae* submissions was a procedural question and that it had the power to admit such submissions under Article 44 of the ICSID Convention.[68] The consistency among these

[64] In this context, the term 'notes' indicates 'how the Tribunal will implement or interpret the UNCITRAL Arbitration Rules, as modified'. See para. 1 of Introduction and Definitions in Appendix B to the Algiers Accords 1981, (1981) 20 ILM 223.

[65] *Methanex*, para. 32. [66] Ibid., para. 33.

[67] Ibid. The Tribunal in *UPS* v. *Canada* reached a substantially similar decision. *United Parcel Service of America Inc* v. *Government of Canada*, UNCITRAL (NAFTA), Decision on *Amici Curiae*, 17 October 2001, available at: http://naftaclaims.com/Disputes/Canada/UPS/UPSDecisionReParticipationAmiciCuriae.pdf.

[68] *Suez, Sociedad General de Aguas de Barcelona, SA and Vivendi Universal, SA* v. *Argentine Republic*, ICSID Case No. ARB/03/19, Order in Response to a Petition for Transparency and Participation as *Amicus Curiae*, 19 May 2005, available at: http://ita.law.uvic.ca/documents/suezMay19EN.pdf. Article 44 of the ICSID Convention reads as follows: 'Any Arbitration proceeding shall be conducted in accordance with the provisions of this Section and, except as the parties otherwise agree, in accordance with the Arbitration

decisions is remarkable given that, except for the Iran-US Tribunal, none of the rules under which the tribunals or the WTO Appellate Body operated provided for *amicus curiae* submissions, and that they all based their decision on residual power in matters of procedure.[69]

The admissibility of *amicus curiae* submissions is predicated on the public interest of the disputes in question and the value of transparency in strengthening the legitimacy of international arbitration. In the words of the ICSID Tribunal:

> Public acceptance of the legitimacy of international arbitral processes, particularly when they involve states and matters of public interest, is strengthened by increased openness and increased knowledge as to how these processes function. It is this imperative that has led to increased transparency in the arbitral processes of the World Trade Organization and the North American Free Trade Agreement. Through the participation of appropriate representatives of civil society in appropriate cases, the public will gain increased understanding of ICSID processes.[70]

It is the sharing of this policy concern among the various tribunals that produced the consistency in their decisions and prompted the statement of the Free Trade Commission. The latest version of the ICSID Arbitration Rules provides that the arbitral tribunal may allow non-disputing parties to file submissions and the procedure to be followed.

3. The interpretation of precedent: *ratio decidendi* and *obiter dicta*

At the theoretical level, since there is no binding precedent there should be no reason to distinguish between *ratio decidendi* and *obiter*

Rules in effect on the date on which the parties consented to arbitration. *If any question of procedure arises which is not covered by this Section or the Arbitration Rules or any rules agreed by the parties, the Tribunal shall decide the question.*' (Emphasis added.)

69 Prior to the case of *Suez, Sociedad General de Aguas de Barcelona, SA and Vivendi Universal, SA* v. *Argentinas*, the *Aguas del Tunari* Tribunal ruled, inter alia, that 'there is not at present a need to call witnesses or seek supplementary non-party submissions at the jurisdictional phase of its work. We hold this view without in anyway prejudging the question of the extent of the Tribunal's authority to call witnesses or receive information from non-parties on its own initiative', *Aguas del Tunari SA* v. *Republic of Bolivia*, ICSID Case No. ARB/02/3, Letter of the President of the Arbitral Tribunal to Mr J.M. Wagner of Earthjustice, 29 January 2003, in reply to a request for his organization and petitioners to join as non-party to the proceedings, available at: http://ita.law.uvic.ca/documents/Aguas-BoliviaResponse.pdf.

70 *Suez, Sociedad General de Aguas de Barcelona, SA and Vivendi Universal, SA* v. *Argentina*, Order, para. 22.

dicta.[71] In practice, however, parties and tribunals argue and reason in terms of precedents. References to *obiter dicta* are not infrequent and are mostly reserved to instances in which the tribunal dismisses as irrelevant the particular finding of another tribunal.[72] By implication, it could be expected that in such cases the tribunal has identified the *ratio decidendi* of the previous decisions cited. This is rarely done and reflects 'the tendency amongst international lawyers of citing dicta from judgments, unqualified by relating them to the facts and the issue; just as if judicial decisions and the comments of writers were *pari passu*'.[73] The ICJ is not immune to such tendencies.[74]

For instance, in *Renta* the Tribunal found alleged precedents to be of 'limited normative applicability' because:

> Quotations of incidental comments are not entitled to be considered as precedents at all; they are not part of the *ratio decidendi* and thus are not part of the reasoning by which the arbitrators fulfill their mandate to decide. That is where they exercise personal responsibility. *Obiter dicta* are commentary. They may be persuasive but are *a priori* of less weight.[75]

[71] 'The absence from international law of any rule of *stare decisis* means that the lawyer should be careful before relying on its ancillary doctrine of the distinction between the *ratio decidendi* and any *obiter dicta*. In one sense, there can be no *obiter dicta* in an international judicial decision. The reason lies in the collective formulation of the decision by all the judges working collegially. In that process, a word or a sentence will be included because a judge thought it necessary and there was no opposition, or if there was opposition the majority decided to include the passage. In that respect, every word is part of the reasoning.' S. Rosenne, 'The Perplexities of Modern International Law: General Course on Public International Law' *Recueil* 291 (2001) 69.

[72] See, for instance, the statement in *Renta* that '[t]he *Berschader* majority thus seems to have relied on a *dictum* which in turn had relied on another *dictum*', *Renta*, 95. See also Broches: 'La question du contrôle direct ou indirect n'était pas déterminante pour la décision du tribunal de rejeter le déclinatoire et les déclarations d'ordre général auxquelles il s'est livré sont des *obiter dicta*' ('The question of direct or indirect control was not determinative in the tribunal rejecting the objection to jurisdiction and the statements of a general nature which it raised are *obiter dicta*'), Declaration by Broches, *Société Ouest Africaine des Bétons Industriels (SOABI) v. State of Senegal*, ICSID Case No. ARB/82/1, 2 ICSID Reports 333, para. 4.

[73] R.Y. Jennings, 'General Course on Principles of International Law', 342–3.

[74] '. . . it must be said that the Court's judgments are not above sometimes citing passages from previous judgments almost as if any pronouncement of the Court may be cited, not because it embodies the decision in the case but because it is a passage that has been hallowed into something akin to the Holy Writ', see Jennings, 'The Judiciary, International and National, and the Development of International Law', 10.

[75] *Renta*, para. 91.

The same Tribunal dismissed *Berschader*'s reliance on *Plama* by observing that the '*Berschader* majority... seems to have relied on a *dictum* which in turn had relied on another *dictum*.'[76]

The determination that the reasoning of a tribunal is *obiter dicta* may be more problematic in the context of ICSID Annulment proceedings, as this determination may result in the annulment of the award for insufficiency of a tribunal's reasoning. In its review of the *CMS* Award, the *ad hoc* Committee observed that:

> Article 27 [of the Articles on State Responsibility] covers cases in which the state of necessity precludes wrongfulness under customary international law. In the present case, the Tribunal rejected Argentina's defense based on state of necessity. Thus Article 27 was not applicable and the paragraphs relating to that Article were *obiter dicta* which could not have any bearing on the operative part of the Award.[77]

As a consequence, it remained to be seen 'on which basis the Tribunal decided that compensation was due by Argentina to CMS for the damage suffered by it from 2000 to 2027'.[78] In this instance, the *ad hoc* Committee found that the Tribunal had already decided on other grounds that Argentina had breached its international obligations and concluded that there was no manifest excess of powers or lack of reasoning in the decision of the Tribunal.[79] However, this case illustrates the reach of the distinction between *ratio decidendi* and *obiter dicta* in annulment proceedings.

The determination of what is or is not a *dictum* may not be an easy exercise for tribunals not schooled in the intricacies of common law judging and are, instead, familiar with legal systems where doctrine may carry more weight than in the common law. Even in common law the distinction between the holding of a case and the remainder of an opinion is elusive, and in the United States judges make less of the distinction than used to be the case.[80] Be that as it may, as explained by Jennings,[81] the discipline required to extract the *ratio decidendi* from a decision and to then relate the extracted statements of legal principle to the facts of the case in the submissions would avoid 'the practice of the casual use of citations from other awards

[76] Ibid., para. 95.
[77] *CMS Gas Transmission Company* v. *Republic of Argentina*, ICSID Case No. ARB/01/8, Decision on Annulment, 25 September 2007, 14 ICSID Reports 251, para. 145.
[78] Ibid., para. 148. [79] Ibid., para. 150.
[80] Posner, *How Judges Think*, 192. Posner attributes this situation to 'the growing influence of pragmatic decision making'.
[81] Jennings, 'General Course on Principles of International Law', 342–3.

without regard to their original contexts',[82] as is evidenced by the usual – and wrong – references made to the *Neer* case.[83]

4. Towards a stronger doctrine of precedent?

As a first step in judging inconsistency, we should be cognizant that investment treaties may be different and may call for different interpretations, even when one of the States parties is the same; moreover, standards such as fair and equitable treatment are, by definition, very fact specific and tribunals may be unaware of certain precedents and the parties, too. Various proposals and ideas have been put forward to address possible inconsistencies, ranging from the establishment of an appellate court to expanding to arbitration the technique of the preliminary consultation of the European Court of Justice. So far none of these proposals have prospered. In the meantime, the following considerations justify tribunals taking a more committed attitude to follow precedent or provide reasons for disregarding it.

First, the granting by States to investors of the right to sue them before arbitral tribunals under Treaties to Promote and Protect Investments is a momentous development. One has only to recall the reluctance of States to accept the compulsory jurisdiction of the ICJ to realize what an extraordinary step this is, which has implications for the onus placed on arbitral tribunals dealing with investment disputes. Second, the fact that States have given an open commitment to arbitrate would also seem to militate in favour of more consistency than would be required (or expected) in *ad hoc* one-shot arbitrations. Investment arbitrations may be 'one-shot arbitrations' for the private party, but not so for the State. It is not only a question of different parties being treated differently by different tribunals: the same State may find that a different interpretation of the law is applied even under the same treaty and on the same set of facts. Third, lack of

[82] See Dissenting Opinion of Cremades in *Fraport AG Frankfurt Airport Services Worldwide* v. *Philippines*, ICSID Case No. ARB/03/25, para. 23, available at: http://ita.law.uvic.ca/documents/FraportAward.pdf. See also comments at para. 24: '[t]he integrity of this interpretative process must not be compromised by the pronouncements of other arbitral tribunals in their interpretation of different treaties in wholly unrelated factual and legal contexts. Other awards or decisions are no more than illustrative of the implications of a standard form of treaty wording'; and para. 23: '[a]s a final point, I refer to the practice of the casual use of citations from other awards without regard to their original contexts. Awards have been cited as if they were authorities or precedents on, for example the significance of illegal conduct by the investor that bear no similarity to the case at issue.'

[83] J. Paulsson and G. Petrochilos, 'Neer-ly Misled?' *ICSID Review* 22 (2007) 242.

an appeals mechanism that may provide unity places more responsibility on the arbitral tribunals to contribute to the certainty and stability of the system. Fourth, certainty and stability of the legal framework are part of the objectives pursued by investment treaties and have been considered part of the standards enshrined in them. Certainty[84] and stability[85] constitute the rationale for a stronger doctrine of precedent.

In the long term – at least for ICSID cases – institutional control mechanisms provided for under the ICSID Convention may contribute 'to the development of a common legal opinion or *jurisprudence constante*, to resolve some difficult legal issues discussed in many cases, inasmuch as these issues share the same substantial features'.[86] But the emergence of a *jurisprudence constante* in this area is a slow process and less certain than in a system based on precedent of individual cases, for it may be difficult to determine when a practice has been established.[87] It is comparable to a river basin where the many rivulets eventually make their way into a single stream. Finding the thread that may unite multiple precedents is an artistic endeavour: 'In his creative role the judge is, indeed, not unlike the poet who respects the inheritance of his native language in the very act of exploiting its resources for novel uses.'[88] It is to be hoped that the creativity of poetic insight may bridge some of the contradictions that have become apparent in the practice of investment tribunals.

[84] Goodhart considered that, as compared with the Continent, the need for certainty – the need for definite fixed rules which shall bind the judges – in England was stronger: 'On the Continent, even before the establishment of the Codes, there was the background of Roman Law which furnished a legal system of developed doctrines and principles. With the codes we get an even stronger framework . . . But in England, the judges had to create this structure almost entirely for themselves, and English justice, if it were not to remain fluid and unstable, required a strong cement. This was found in the common law doctrine of precedent with its essential and peculiar emphasis on rigidity and certainty', A.L. Goodhart, *Precedent in English and Continental Law* (London: Stevens and Sons, 1934), 3–4.

[85] 'probably the main force behind the doctrine of precedent is that in a system of case law, adherence to precedent is necessary to create the kind of stability that one would have in a system in which law was codified', Posner, *How Judges Think*, 144.

[86] *AES* v. *Argentina*, 33.

[87] Goodhart, *Precedent in English and Continental Law*, 43. It requires 'a sufficient degree of clarity, continuity and permanence', Guillaume 'The Use of Precedent by International Judges and Arbitrators', 6.

[88] Fuller, *Anatomy of the Law*, 136.

8

Publicists

Article 38(1)(d) of the ICJ Statute authorizes the Court to apply the writings of 'most highly qualified publicists', besides judicial decisions, as subsidiary means to determine the rules of law.[1] The ICJ has made scant use of this subsidiary means other than by general references such as 'almost universal opinion' or 'all or nearly all writers'.[2] This has been attributed to the process of collective drafting and to avoid the selection of citations.[3] Other international tribunals, and certainly arbitral tribunals established pursuant to investment treaties, make generous use of doctrine. Historically such use had been influenced by the unavailability of published primary sources and the difficulty to interpret them.[4]

[1] Statute of the International Court of Justice, 26 June 1945, 33 UNTS 99, Article 38(1)(d) states that: 'subject to the provisions of Article 59, judicial decisions and the teachings of the most highly qualified publicists of the various nations, as subsidiary means for the determination of rules of law'.

[2] For a list, see I. Brownlie, *Principles of International Law* (7th edn, Oxford University Press, 2008), 24, footnote 154. However, Brownlie points out that: 'The fact that writers are used by the Court is evidenced by the dissenting opinions in which the "workings" are set out in more detail and reflect the actual methods of the approach of the Court as a whole', ibid., 24.

[3] Ibid.

[4] 'The precise content of international law was for so long so uncertain and so difficult to establish, the rules comprising it so sparse and ineffectual, and the number familiar with them so limited that the works of those writers who had devoted themselves to this little known branch of law afforded the principal, and indeed almost the only, sources of information concerning it. It was all the more necessary to resort to them so long as it was universally conceded that, in the absence of established positive rules, recourse might be had to natural law and Roman law as sources of international law; but these, and the former especially, were only accessible in the works of the publicists', M. Virally,

While published sources such as treaties, State practice and judicial decisions have exponentially increased in the past decades, their interpretation by 'highly qualified publicists' continues to be referred to,[5] and notwithstanding the variety of opinions which may be encountered, these references to the writings of scholars may have a unifying effect. It is not intended here to conduct a review of all extant arbitral decisions and their use of doctrine,[6] but a few examples will be given to show the impact of the writings of publicists in investment arbitration and their influence in shaping case law.

The influence of doctrine may decline as judicial activity and its publication increases.[7] However, the usefulness of the scholarly critical work on judicial activity remains relevant. In deploring the avalanche of decisions by tribunals great and small in the United States, Cardozo commented that the great number of cases produced a situation where citation of precedent tended to count for less and the resulting perplexity of the judge became the scholar's opportunity: 'More and more we are looking to the scholar in his study, to the jurist rather than to the judge or lawyer for inspiration and

'The Sources of International Law' in M. Sørensen (ed.), *Manual of Public International Law* (London: Macmillan, 1968), 153.

5 '[I]nternational law still remains, in many of its aspects, difficult to discover or interpret. The researches of scholars continue, therefore, to be useful not only for the ascertainment of the positive law, but also as guidance for its development and as a means of filling its deficiencies', ibid. See further comments by Lauterpacht: 'While the availability of other sources of information may have altered the nature of the function of "publicists" as recorders of the practice of States, their part as its qualified interpreters cannot always be disregarded', H. Lauterpacht, *Development of International Law by the International Court, being a revised edition of The Development of International Law by the Permanent Court of International Justice* (London: Stevens, 1958), 25.

6 This has been done by J.F. Commission in 'Precedent in Investment Treaty Arbitration: the Empirical Backing' *TDM* (2007) 4(5), see under 'Other Sources Cited' in Tables A, B and C.

7 According to Pellet: 'It is not illogical that the weight of the legal doctrine, so eminently influential in laying the foundations of international law, decreases with the growth of international judicial activity, the development of the case law of the Court and the new means to get knowledge of State practice', A. Pellet, 'Article 38', in A. Zimmermann, C. Tomuschat and K. Oellers-Frahm (eds.), *The Statute of the International Court of Justice: A Commentary* (Oxford University Press, 2006), 677, 791. Sir Henry Maine's lectures on International Law delivered at Cambridge University in 1887, for instance, referred only to the *Alabama Claims* case, see H. Maine, *A Series of Lectures Delivered before the University of Cambridge, 1887* (New York: Henry Holt and Company, 1888). For Jennings, there were many cases on international law already decided, but 'there was until relatively recent times no international lawyers' *apparatus technicus* to make cases accessible as material for argument', R.Y. Jennings, 'General Course on Principles of International Law' *Recueil* 121 (1967) 323, 342.

for guidance.'[8] The frequent citation of and reliance by arbitral tribunals on Schreuer's analysis of the ICSID Convention stands as proof of it.[9]

An instance of reliance on scholarly analysis of case law can be found in the award in *Pantechniki.* On the basis of the analysis of Douglas in *The International Law of Investment Claims*, the sole arbitrator rejected as a jurisdictional test the list of characteristics of an investment set forth in *Salini* without referring to the long line of awards which have dealt with the concept of investment. The arbitrator agreed with the author that the so-called *Salini* test left a wide margin of subjective appreciation of what is an investment. Douglas had said that: '[i]f the fundamental objective is to attract capital, then the concept of an investment cannot be one in search of meaning in the pleadings submitted to an investment treaty tribunal that is established years, perhaps decades, after the decision to commit capital to the host state was made.'[10] The arbitrator considered that Rule 23 proposed by Douglas, which excludes 'a certain duration' and 'contribution to the host state's development' as excessively subjective, may well encapsulate an emerging synthesis.[11]

[8] B. Cardozo, *The Growth of the Law* (New Haven, Conn.: Yale University Press, 1924), 6, 11. Paulsson and Petrochilos's article on the misapplication of the *Neer* case is illustrative of the usefulness of doctrinal analysis: J. Paulsson and G. Petrochilos, '*Neer*-ly Missed?' *ICSID Review* 22 (2007) 242. This article concludes: 'There should be no doubt that, to the extent the customary-law minimum standard has any role to play in the interpretation of investment treaties, the *Neer* formula is of limited import. The majority of modern claims concern administrative or legislative acts, which in the United States-Mexico General Claims Commission's classification are to be regarded as cases of direct responsibility where the alleged injury flows directly from such acts. *Neer* was on its own terms inapplicable in such cases – in 1926 and a fortiori today. In customary law, those acts would properly fall to be measured by the Roberts formula of treatment "in accordance with ordinary standards of civilization". That, not *Neer*'s, is therefore the formulation which needs to be understood, developed, or indeed reconsidered in the context of investment protection', at 257. Cf. *Glamis Gold, Ltd.* v. *The United States of America*, UNCITRAL Award, 8 June 2009, available at: www.state.gov/documents/organization/125798.pdf.

[9] See references to Gaillard's yearly commentary on ICSID decisions and awards, published in the *Journal du Droit international* since 1986. These commentaries are now consolidated in E. Gaillard, *La Jurisprudence du CIRDI* (Paris: Pédone, 2004), vol. I with case law from 1965 to 2003, and E. Gaillard, *La Jurisprudence du CIRDI* (Paris: Pédone, 2010), vol. II with case law from 2004 to 2008.

[10] Z. Douglas, *The International Law of Investment Claims* (Cambridge University Press, 2009), 190.

[11] *Pantechniki SA Contractors & Engineers* v. *Republic of Albania*, ICSID Case No. ARB/07/21, Award, 30 July 2009, para. 36, available at: http://icsid.worldbank.org/ICSID. Rule 23 reads as follows: 'The economic materialization of an investment requires the commitment of resources to the economy of the host state by the claimant entailing the assumption of risk in expectation of a commercial return', Douglas, *The International Law of Investment Claims*, 189.

In the same award, the level of State vigilance required in a situation of civil unrest or rebellion was addressed from the perspective of the *Cutler* case and by reference to the view expressed by O'Connell in his treatise on *International Law*. According to the sole arbitrator, his review of cases *and doctrine* led him to follow the reasoning of O'Connell and to 'adopt the more recent conclusion of Newcombe and Paradell in *Law and Practice of Investment Treaties*';[12] no specific reference to precedents of the BIT generation may be found in the award.

Occasionally, a form of dialogue may take place between a Tribunal and a writer when, in the opinion of the writer, a Tribunal misreads his opinion. For instance, the sole arbitrator in *Malaysian Historical Salvors* understood Schreuer's analysis of the case law on the issue of whether a contribution of an investment to the host State's economic development was a jurisdictional element of the concept of investment to mean that such contribution was a mandatory requirement.[13] The authors of the subsequent edition of *The ICSID Convention: A Commentary* considered the development from a descriptive list of typical features of what constitutes an investment towards a set of mandatory legal requirements to be unfortunate, and stated that the 'First Edition of this Commentary cannot serve as authority for this development'.[14]

Besides critical analysis of arbitration awards, the effect of writings on the reasoning of arbitral tribunals may also take a more indirect form. Investment treaty arbitration is followed closely by a substantial academic community which, with its critical comments, may shape public opinion's view of the system and, in turn, affect the reasoning of tribunals. In *Methanex*, the concern of the Tribunal to be perceived to be 'secretive', as opposed to 'more open or transparent',[15] influenced its decision to receive *amicus curiae* submissions.

The individual opinions of judges deserve separate mention. They have been considered to be halfway between judicial decisions and opinions of

[12] *Pantechniki*, para. 81, citing A. Newcombe and L. Paradell, *Law and Practice of Investment Treaties* (The Netherlands: Kluwer Law International, 2009), 310.

[13] *Malaysian Historical Salvors, SDN, BHD* v. *Malaysia*, ICSID Case No. ARB/05/10, Decision on Jurisdiction, 17 May 2007, paras. 67–8, available at: http://icsid.worldbank.org/ICSID/.

[14] C. Shreuer *et al.*, *The ICSID Convention: A Commentary* (2nd edn, Cambridge University Press, 2009), 133.

[15] *Methanex* v. *United States*, UNCITRAL (NAFTA), Decision on Petitions from Third Persons to Intervene as 'Amici Curiae', 15 January 2001, 7 ICSID Reports 224, para. 49.

publicists,[16] in part because these opinions are written after hearing the parties' arguments and 'the attempt to apply principles and rules to real situations both demonstrates and illuminates the law in a way that is usually more convincing than abstract commentary however skilled'.[17] In arbitral practice we find, for instance, frequent references to the opinion of Judge Higgins in the *Oil Platforms* case in respect of the level of proof necessary for an arbitral tribunal to decide on its own jurisdiction.[18] However, in the cases of *ad hoc* tribunals of limited membership and of jurisdictions where the majority of members of the tribunal have usually been appointed by the parties, the authority of individual opinions should be viewed with caution. An analysis of dissenting opinions in ICSID decisions up to 2008 shows that, in most instances, their author is the arbitrator appointed by the losing party.[19]

However, in contested areas of the law, the dissenting opinion of an arbitrator may be referred to, or even its reasoning adopted unanimously in a subsequent award, irrespective of who appointed the arbitrator. For example, in the context of the interpretation of the MFN clause, the jurisdictional award in *RosInvest* took note of, among many others, the *Berschader* award and of the appended dissenting opinion to that award, without entering into a detailed discussion of either of them.[20] Subsequently, the *Renta* award

[16] Virally confers this status only on the separate and dissenting opinions of judges of the ICJ, see Virally, 'The Sources of International Law', 153–4.

[17] According to Jennings, for this reason judicial decisions carry more weight than writers' opinions, see Jennings, 'General Course on Principles of International Law', 342. This comment can be applied to individual opinions of members of a tribunal as well.

[18] See *Desert Line Projects LLC* v. *Yemen*, ICSID Case No. ARB/05/17, Award, 6 February 2008, paras. 129 ff, and other examples cited there. According to H. Lauterpacht: 'The degree of their [individual opinions'] intrinsic merit will determine in every case the permanence of their place in the development of international law and in the comprehension of the decisions of the Court', *Development of International Law*, 70.

[19] A.J. van den Berg, 'Dissenting Opinions by Party-Appointed Arbitrators in Investment Arbitration', draft dated 31 August 2009, on file with the author. These results match those of international commercial arbitration. See A. Redfern, 'Dissenting Opinions in International Commercial Arbitration' *Arbitration International* 20 (2004) 223. The adjective 'individual' may not reflect accurately the nature of an opinion which, irrespective of the title, may in substance be a dissenting opinion. For clarity's sake, the adjective 'dissenting' is used based on the content of the opinion, even when it bears the title of 'Individual Opinion'.

[20] *RosInvestCo UK Ltd* v. *The Russian Federation*, SCC Case No. Arb V079/2005, Award on Jurisdiction, October 2007, paras. 136–7, available at: http://ita.law.uvic.ca/documents/RosInvestjurisdiction_decision_2007_10_001.pdf. Weiler gave its opinion in *Berschader* the title of 'separate opinion', even when he dissented. See the opinion appended to the award at: http://ita.law.uvic.ca/documents/BerschaderFinalAward.pdf.

on Preliminary Questions quoted relevant parts of the *RosInvest* award and noted that the reasoning was similar to that of the dissenting opinion in *Berschader*.[21]

In another contested area, that of the determination of 'foreign control' under Article 25(2)(b) of the ICSID Convention, the Tribunal in *TSA* v. *Argentina* pointed out that the interpretation of this article by the *Rompetrol* and *Tokios Tokelės* Tribunals had not been followed and had been criticized by Weil, president of the latter Tribunal.[22] It then refused to stop short of the second corporate layer in establishing foreign control and proceeded to pursue 'its objective identification of foreign control up to its real source, using the same criterion with which it started'.[23] In other less controversial matters, reference may be made to general statements found in a dissenting opinion because of their intrinsic value and the standing of the arbitrator: *Glamis Gold*, for example, quoted extensively from Wälde's observations on the respect owed to precedent.[24]

Tribunals usually do not discuss the basis for the authority of the views of writers, judges or arbitrators cited in their decisions or their relative authority vis-à-vis each other. There would be a certain inconsistency in the use of subsidiary means to establish the law if a tribunal dismisses *obiter dicta* of another tribunal as being just an opinion or commentary and then relies on writers' opinions. Judicial decisions, publicists' writings and ICJ judges' opinions are often quoted side by side. For instance, in the *Eureko* award, the Tribunal made extensive doctrinal references on a particular issue – the interpretation of an umbrella clause – before it engaged in

21 *Renta 4 SVSA et al* v. *Russian Federation*, SCC No. 24/2007, Award on Preliminary Objections, 20 March 2009, para. 98, available at: http://ita.law.uvic.ca/documents/Renta.pdf.

22 The *Rompetrol* award dismissed Weil's dissenting opinion: 'The Tribunal (which is not, of course, bound by the decisions of other ICSID tribunals) can leave aside the question what authority should be attached to a dissenting opinion in contrast to the Award itself, since (as the Claimant argued) the view expressed by Prof. Weil has not been widely approved in the academic and professional literature, or generally adopted by subsequent tribunals. The Tribunal would in any case have great difficulty in an approach that was tantamount to setting aside the clear language agreed upon by the treaty Parties in favor of a wide-ranging policy discussion', *The Rompetrol Group NV* v. *Romania*, ICSID Case No. ARB/06/3, Decision on Jurisdiction and Admissibility, 18 April 2008, para. 85, available at: http://icsid.worldbank.org/ICSID/.

23 *TSA Spectrum de Argentina, SA* v. *Argentina*, ICSID Case No. ARB/05/5, Award, 19 December 2008, para. 147, available at: http://ita.law.uvic.ca/documents/TSAAwardEng_000.pdf.

24 *Glamis Gold, Ltd.* v. *The United States of America*, UNCITRAL Award, 8 June 2009, 5 (para. 7), available at: www.state.gov/documents/organization/125798.pdf.

the consideration of the relevant practice of other tribunals.[25] Since it is rare that tribunals engage in doctrinal discussion, references to writings or opinions may be limited to those that support the tribunal's view of the issue discussed.

Expert institutions such as the Institute of International Law and in particular the International Law Commission (ILC), make a substantial contribution to the consistency of the law in their respective areas of concern. Suffice here to say that the Articles on State Responsibility adopted by the ILC are without doubt the most often-quoted document in investment treaty arbitral decisions and have assisted in the development of consistent case law, although arbitrators' need for guidance has led them to apply the Articles to issues to which they do not apply or 'to apply them beyond the terms of the ILC's text'.[26]

To conclude, only the opinions of a limited number of writers, judges or arbitrators can be said to assist tribunals to decide more consistently. We cannot count on a Law of Citations,[27] by naming as primary authorities the equivalents of Papinian, Paul, Ulpian, Modestinus and Gaius. If their opinions differed, the majority view was to be followed. If the numbers were equal, Papinian's view prevailed. If the numbers were equal and Papinian was silent, the judge could make up his own mind on the matter.[28] The lack of emperors with such powers has been replaced by the recognition by counsel and arbitral tribunals of the quality of scholarship and cogency of reasoning of those few who become 'highly respected publicists'. A more consensus-based procedure than provided by imperial authority in the Roman system, but a more prolonged process with a less certain outcome.

[25] *Eureko BV* v. *Republic of Poland, ad hoc* Arbitration, Partial Award, 19 August 2005, 12 ICSID Reports 331, para. 251.

[26] See J. Crawford, 'Similarity of Issues in Disputes Arising under the Same or Similarly Drafted Investment Treaties' in E. Gaillard and Y. Banifatemi (eds.), *Precedent in International Arbitration* (New York: Juris Publishing, 2008), 100.

[27] Law of AD 426 in the names of Emperor Theodosius II and Valentinian III.

[28] P. Stein, *Roman Law in European History* (Cambridge University Press, 2005), 28.

Conclusion

Uncertainty is not limited to international investment law or international law. It is common to many areas of the law.[1] Nonetheless, what is specific to international arbitration of investment disputes between investors and States is that States have consented to arbitrate future disputes before *ad hoc* arbitral tribunals and to be judged against standards of elusive content. The uncertainty is at two levels: the substantive content of the standards and the *ad hoc* nature of the arbitral tribunals.

By their nature, *ad hoc* tribunals may be inclined just to settle the dispute and be less concerned with 'the shape and direction'[2] of investment law. There is a contradiction between the granting to *ad hoc* arbitral tribunals of the wide discretion that BIT standards entail and expecting consistency in their decisions. Nonetheless, arbitral tribunals to a certain extent have shown concern for the future shape and direction of the law, since publication of their decisions and awards has exposed the differences in how tribunals qualify facts and understand the law.

In wondering what would happen if judicial decisions were not made public, Atiyah considered that the courts would focus on the past and the present position of the parties and the judicial process would become

[1] 'uncertainty is not a problem bedeviling only international law. One is reminded of the index to H.L.A. Hart's famous book, *The Concept of Law*. The item reads, "Certainty of Law. See Uncertainty".' W. Michael Reisman, 'The Supervisory Jurisdiction of the International Court of Justice', Introduction, fn. 6. Richard Posner considers uncertainty 'a fundamental characteristic of the U.S. legal system', *How Judges Think*, 35.

[2] R.Y. Jennings, 'Chambers of the International Court of Justice and Courts of Arbitration' in *Humanité et Droit International. Mélanges René-Jean Dupuy* (Paris: Éditions A. Pedone, 1991), 200.

a sort of arbitration process.[3] In the case of investment arbitration, we are in the presence of a reverse situation, and it is symptomatic that as a consequence of publicity the literature on precedent and arbitration has grown exponentially in recent years and that we find with some frequency in the awards statements of 'policy' in respect of precedents.

At the same time, tribunals tend to find a breach of the standard of fair and equitable treatment, the most undetermined of the standards in a BIT, in preference to any other standard of protection. A consequence of the emphasis on the particular circumstances of the case translates into fact-specific awards and their diminished value as precedents. This tendency may have other consequences for the arbitral process itself, since fact-specific awards are hardly suitable for appeal mechanisms,[4] which have been discussed, but so far not prospered.

The tendency towards standards of fairness or reasonableness based on the overall circumstances of the case is not unique to arbitral tribunals deciding investment disputes and has parallels in contemporary domestic law:

> Even where the general shape of the substantive legal rules has not significantly altered, there has been a profound shift away from principles to pragmatism, a shift from the desire to lay down rules for future application to the desire to do justice according to the particular circumstances of the case . . . It is scarcely possible today to open a Statute conferring jurisdiction upon the courts without finding instances of rules qualified by some discretion.[5]

The choice of the standard with the largest measure of discretion implies a proportionate effort to justify it, if the exercise of the discretion is to remain legitimate. Thomas Franck drew attention to the paradox that results from the introduction of a fairness standard in a rule because the indeterminacy of the concept may affect the legitimacy of the rule itself. In his view, '[t]his

[3] 'What would surely happen then is that the courts would focus on the past and the present to the exclusion of the future; they would tend to concentrate exclusively on what *has* happened, and on the present position of the parties, and impose a solution which appears to them to be the most appropriate solution in all the circumstances of the case. This would naturally lead to the judicial process becoming converted into a sort of arbitration process, a process in which law and principle are largely discarded except in so far as they serve the function of assisting in arriving at an equitable solution', 'From Principles to Pragmatism: Changes in the Function of the Judicial Process and the Law' *Iowa L. Rev.* 65 (1980) 1249. Emphasis in original.

[4] Ibid., 1271. [5] Ibid., 1255.

conundrum cannot be resolved; it can only be managed by the persuasive quality of discourse'.[6]

The quality of the discourse could be improved. Motivation between different interpretative approaches to the same treaty clause may remain inarticulate. A text may be subject to wide or narrow interpretation as if it were an accordion.[7] The preamble to the ICSID Convention's objective to support foreign investment is ignored when it comes to origin of funds. On the other hand, reference to international cooperation for economic development at times has been expanded to require that an investment contribute to economic development to qualify as such under the ICSID Convention. The MFN clause may be interpreted restrictively while amplifying the exceptions. Reference to the Vienna Convention has become a ritual step before proceeding in ways which may not be congruent with it. Statements of policy on precedents may not be applied in the very award where they are made.[8]

The quality of the discourse means that the choice between conflicting principles and contentions, in Sir Hersch Lauterpacht's own words, 'can be made only after conscientious and exhaustive scrutiny; even then the decision, when made, is not invariably accompanied by any feeling of inevitability. The only sentiment that can be registered with confidence is that the decision is accompanied by a consciousness of duty performed.'[9]

6 T.M. Franck, *Fairness in International Law and Institutions* (Oxford: Clarendon Press, 1995), 34.

7 The importance of interpreting a term in its context is graphically expressed by the Appellate Body of the WTO in referring to the meaning of 'like' in 'like products': the interpretation of this term 'is a discretionary decision that must be made in considering the various characteristics of products in individual cases . . . The concept of "likeness" is a relative one that evokes the image of an accordion. The accordion of "likeness" stretches and squeezes in different places as different provisions of the WTO Agreement are applied.' *Japan–Alcoholic Beverages*, WT/DS38/AB/R, para. 8.5.

8 A fact not uncommon in municipal law: '. . . whereas much or most of what is commonly written about precedent takes as its raw material what judges have said about precedent, I propose to take as mine, not so much what they have *said* as what they have *done* about it.' K.N. Llewellyn, *The Bramble Bush* (Oxford University Press, 2008), 65.

9 *Development of International Law*, 396.

Bibliography

Arsanjani, M.H. and Reisman, W. Michael, 'Interpreting Treaties for the Benefit of Third Parties: The "Salvors Doctine" and the Use of Legislative History in Investment Treaties' *AJIL* (2010) 104 597.

Atiyah, P.S. and Summers, R.S., *Form and Substance in Anglo-American Law. A Comparative Study of Legal Reasoning, Legal Theory and Legal Institutions* (Oxford: Clarendon Press, repr. 2002).

Atiyah, P.S., 'Judges and Policy' *Israel L. Rev.* 15 (1980) 346.

'From Principles to Pragmatism: Changes in the Function of the Judicial Process and the Law' *Iowa L. Rev.* 65 (1980) 1249.

Aust, A., *Modern Treaty Law and Practice* (2nd edn, Cambridge University Press, 2007).

Baker, J.H., *An Introduction to English Legal History* (4th edn, London: Butterworths, 2002).

Barak, A., *Purposive Interpretation in Law* (Princeton University Press, 2005).

Bedjaoui, M., 'L'opportunité dans les decisions de la Cour Internationale de Justice' in Laurence Boisson de Chazournes and Vera Gowlland-Debbas (eds.), *The International Legal System in Quest of Equity and Universality: Liber Amicorum Georges Abi-Saab* (The Hague: Martinus Nijhoff Publishers, 2001).

Bell, J., *Policy Arguments in Judicial Decisions* (Oxford: Clarendon Press, 1983).

Brierly, J.L., 'The Basis of Obligation in International Law' in H. Lauterpacht and C.H.M. Waldock (eds.), *The Basis of Obligation in International Law and Other Papers by the Late James Leslie Brierly* (Oxford: Clarendon Press, 1958).

Broches, A., *Selected Essays: World Bank, ICSID, and other Subjects of Public and Private International Law* (Dordrecht: Nijhoff, 1995).

Brownlie, I., 'Treatment of Aliens: Assumption of Risk and the International Standard' in W. Flume, H.J. Hahn, G. Kegel and K.R. Simmonds, *International Law and Economic Order: Essays in Honour of F.A. Mann* (Munich: Verlag C.H. Beck, 1977).

Principles of Public International Law (6th edn, Oxford University Press, 2003).

Buergenthal, T., 'The Proliferation of Disputes, Dispute Settlement Procedures and Respect for the Rule of Law' *ICSID Rev.* 21 (2006) 126.

Burdeau, G., 'Le pouvoir créateur de la jurisprudence internationale à l'épreuve de la dispersion des juridictions' in *La création du droit par le juge Archives de philosophie du droit* 50 (2007) 289–304.
Cardozo, B., *The Growth of the Law* (New Haven, Conn.: Yale University Press, 1924).
Cheng, B., *General Principles of Law as Applied by International Courts and Tribunals* (repr., Cambridge University Press, 2006).
Chinkin, C. and Boyle, A., *The Making of International Law* (Oxford University Press, 2007).
Commission, J.P., 'Precedent in Investment Treaty Arbitration' *Journal of International Arbitration* 24 (2007) 129.
Crawford, J., *The International Law Commission's Articles on State Responsibility. Introduction, Text and Commentaries* (Cambridge University Press, 2002).
'Treaty and Contract in Investment Arbitration' *Arbitration International* 24 (2008) 351.
'Similarity of Issues in Disputes Arising under the Same or Similarly Drafted Investment Treaties' in E. Gaillard and Y. Banifatemi (eds.), *The Precedent in International Arbitration* (Paris: IAI, 2008).
de Visscher, C., *Theory and Reality in Public International Law* (Princeton University Press, 1957).
Problèmes d'interpretation judiciaire en droit international public (Paris: Pédone, 1963).
Denza, E. and Brooks, S., 'Investment Protection Treaties: United Kingdom Experience' *ICLQ* 36 (1987) 908.
Douglas, Z., 'The Hybrid Foundations of Investment Treaty Arbitration' *BYIL* 74 (2004) 151.
The International Law of Investment Claims (Cambridge University Press, 2009).
Farber, D.A. and Sherry, S., *Judgment Calls* (Oxford University Press, 2009).
Fitzmaurice, G., 'Some Problems Regarding the Formal Sources of International Law' in *Symbolae Verzjil: Présentées au professeur J. H. W. Verzijl à l'occasion de son LXXX-ième anniversaire* (The Hague: Martinus Nijhoff, 1958).
Fortier, L.Y. and Drymer, S.L., 'Indirect Expropriation in the Law of International Investment: I Know It When I See It, or *Caveat Investor*' *ICSID Rev.* 19 (2004) 326.
Franck, T.M., *Fairness in International Law and Institutions* (Oxford: Clarendon Press, 1995).
Friedmann, W., 'Legal Philosophy and Judicial Lawmaking' *Colum. L. R.* 61 (1961) 821.
Fuller, L., *Anatomy of the Law* (Harmondsworth: Penguin Books, 1968).
Gaillard, E., *La jurisprudence du CIRDI* Vol. I (2004) and Vol. II (2004–8) (Paris: Éditions Pedone).
and Y. Banifatemi (eds.), *The Precedent in International Arbitration* (Paris: IAI, 2008).
Goodhart, A.L., *Precedent in English and Continental Law* (London: Stevens and Sons, 1934).
Gros, L., 'La recherche du consensus dans les décisions de la Cour Internationale de Justice' in Rudolf Bernhardt (ed.), *Völkerrecht als Rechtsordnung, internationale Gerichtsbarkeit, Menschenrechte: Festschrift für Hermann Mosler* (Berlin: Springer, 1983) 358.

Guillaume, G., 'The Use of Precedent by International Judges and Arbitrators' *Journal of International Dispute Settlement* 2 (2011) 5–23.

Jennings, R.Y., 'General Course on Principles of International Law' *Recueil des cours* (1967) 121.

'Chambers of the International Court of Justice and Courts of Arbitration' in *Humanité et Droit International. Mélanges René-Jean Dupuy* (Paris: Éditions A. Pedone, 1991) 200.

'The Judiciary, International and National, and the Development of International Law' *ICLQ* 45 (1996) 4.

Jiménez Piernas, C., *La conducta arriesgada en la responsabilidad internacional de los estados* (Universidad de Alicante, 1988).

Kaufmann-Kohler, G., 'Is Consistency a Myth?' in Gaillard and Banifatemi (eds.), *Precedent in International Arbitration* 145.

Koskenniemi, M., *From Apology to Utopia* (Cambridge University Press, 2005).

Kratochwil, F.V., *Rules, Norms and Decisions: On the Conditions of Practical and Legal Reasoning in International Relations and Domestic Affairs* (Cambridge University Press, 1989).

Kriebaum, U., 'Privatizing Human Rights. The Interface Between International Investment Protection and Human Rights' *TDM* 3(5) (2006).

Lachs, M., 'Some Reflections on Substance and Form in International Law' in W. Friedmann, L. Henkin and O. Lissitzyn (eds.), *Transnational Law in a Changing Society. Essays in Honor of Philip C. Jessup* (New York: Columbia University Press, 1972) 112.

Lalive, P., 'The First World Bank Arbitration (*Holiday Inns v Morocco*) – Some Legal Problems' *BYBIL* 51 (1980) 123.

Lauterpacht, E., 'The Development of the Law of International Organization by the Decisions of International Tribunals' *Recueil des cours* 152 (1976) 377–478.

Lauterpacht, H., *The Function of Law in the International Community* (Oxford: Clarendon Press, 1933).

The Development of International Law by the International Court (London: Stevens, 1958).

Lewis, T. Ellis, 'The History of Judicial Precedent' *LQR* 48 (1932) 230.

Lindquist, S. and Cross, F., 'Empirically Testing Dworkin's Chain Novel Theory' *NYU L. Rev.* 80 (2005) 1156.

Lowe, V., 'The Politics of Law-Making: Are the Method and Character of Norm Creation Changing?' in M. Byers (ed.), *The Role of Law in International Politics* (Oxford University Press, 2000) 207–26.

'Shareholders' Rights to Control and Manage: From *Barcelona Traction* to *ELSI*' in N. Ando, E. McWhinney and R. Wolfrum (eds.), *Liber Amicorum Judge Shigeru Oda* (The Hague: Kluwer Law International, 2002).

Lozano Contreras, F., *La noción de diligencia debida en derecho internacional público* (Barcelona: Atelier, 2007).

MacCormick, N., *Legal Reasoning and Legal Theory* (Oxford: Clarendon Press, 1978).

Mclachlan, C., 'Principle of Systemic Integration and Article 31(3)(c) of the Vienna Convention' *ICLQ* 54 (2005) 279.

Mason, E.S. and Asher, R.E., *The World Bank since Bretton Woods* (Washington DC: Brookings Institution Press, 1973).

Merrils, J.G., *The Development of International Law by the European Court of Human Rights* (2nd edn, Manchester University Press, 1993).
Moore, J.B., *International Arbitrations* (Washington DC: Government Printing Office, 1898).
Newcombe, A. and Paradell, L., *Law Practice of Investment Treaties. Standards of Treatment* (The Netherlands: Kluwer Law International, 2009).
Nieto, A., *El arbitrio judicial* (2nd edn, Barcelona: Editorial Ariel, 2007).
Paulsson, J., 'International Arbitration and the Generation of Legal Norms: Treaty Arbitration and International Law' *TDM* 3(5) (2006) 2.
'Moral Hazard in International Dispute Resolution', 7, available at: www.arbitration-icca.org/media/0/12773749999020/paulsson_moral_hazard.pdf.
and Petrochilos, G., 'Neer-ly Missled', *ICSID Review – FILJ* 22 (2007) 242.
Pellet, A., 'Article 38', in A. Zimmermann, C. Tomuschat and K. Oellers-Frahm (eds.), *The Statute of the International Court of Justice: A Commentary* (Oxford University Press, 2006) 677.
Posner, R., *How Judges Think* (Cambridge, Mass.: Harvard University Press, 2008).
Redfern, A., 'Dissenting Opinions in International Commercial Arbitration' *Arbitration International* 20 (2004) 223.
Reisman, W.M., 'The Supervisory Jurisdiction of the International Court of Justice: International Arbitration and International Adjudication' *Recueil des cours* 258 (1996).
'International Investment Arbitration and ADR: Married but Best Living Apart' *ICSID Rev.* 24 (2009).
Rigo Sureda, A., 'Investment and Economic Development' in M.A. Fernández-Ballesteros and D. Arias Lozano (eds.), *Liber Amicorum Bernardo Cremades* (Madrid: La Ley, 2010) 1033–46.
Robertson, D., *Judicial Discretion in the House of Lords* (Oxford: Clarendon Press, 1998).
Rosenne, S., 'Some Thoughts on International Arbitration Today' *Israel L. Rev.* 27 (1993).
'The Perplexities of Modern International Law: General Course on Public International Law' *Recueil des cours* 291 (2001).
Rubins, N., '*Loewen v United States*: The Burial of an Investor-State Arbitration Claim' *Arbitration International* 21 (2005) 1.
Salmon, J., 'Quelques observations sur la qualification en droit international public' in C. Perelman and P. Foriers (eds.), *La motivation des décisions de justice* (Brussels: Bruylant, 1978).
Schneiderman, D., 'Judicial Politics and International Investment Arbitration: Seeking an Explanation for Conflicting Outcomes,' 15. Available at: http://works.bepress.com/david_schneiderman/.
Schønberg, S., *Legitimate Expectations in Administrative Law* (Oxford University Press, 2000).
Schreuer, C., 'Fair and Equitable Treatment in Arbitral Practice' *The Journal of World Investment & Trade* 6 (2005) 357.
et al. The ICSID Convention. A Commentary (2nd edn, Cambridge University Press, 2009).

and M. Weiniger, 'Conversations across Cases – Is There a Doctrine of Precedent in Investment Arbitration?' *TDM* 5(3) (2008) 8.
Schwebel, S. 'The Majority Vote of an International Arbitral Tribunal' in *Justice in International Law: Selected Writings of Stephen M. Schwebel* (Cambridge University Press, 2008), 213–22.
'The Proliferation of International Tribunals: Threat or Promise?' in V. Lowe and M. Fitzmaurice (eds.), *Fifty Years of the International Court of Justice: Essays in Honour of Sir Robert Jennings* (Cambridge University Press, 2007) 3.
Shahabuddeen, M., *Precedent in the World Court* (Cambridge University Press, 1996).
Sinclair, A., Nationality Requirements for Investors in ICSID Arbitration: The Award in *Soufraki* v. *The United Arab Emirates*, available at: http://ita.law.uvic.ca/documents/CommentonSoufraki.pdf.
Sinclair, I., *The Vienna Convention on the Law of Treaties* (2nd edn, Manchester University Press, 1984).
Sorel, J.M., 'Interprétation des traités' in O. Corten and P. Klein (eds.), *Les conventions de Vienne sur le droit des traités: commentaire article par article*, vol. II (Brussels: Bruylant, 2006).
Stern, B., 'Are Some Issues Too Political to Be Arbitrable?' *ICSID Rev.* 24 (2009).
Stone, J., 'Fictitional Elements in Treaty Interpretation – A Study in the International Judicial Process' *Sydney L. Rev.* 1(3) (1954) 344.
Sunstein, C.R., *Legal Reasoning and Political Conflict* (New York: Oxford University Press, 1996).
Sweet, A.S. and McCrown, M., 'Discretion and Precedent in European Law' in O. Wiklund (ed.), *Judicial Discretion in European Perspective* (The Hague: Kluwer Law International, 2003).
Tudor, I., *The Fair and Equitable Treatment Standard in the International Law of Foreign Investment* (Oxford University Press, 2008).
Tupman, W.M., 'Case Studies in the Jurisdiction of ICSID' *ICLQ* 35 (1986) 813.
van den Berg, A.J., 'Dissenting Opinions by Party-Appointed Arbitrators in Investment Arbitration' in M.H. Arsanjani *et al.* (eds.), *Looking to the Future. Essays on International law in Honor of W. Michael Reisman* (Leiden and Boston: Martinus Nijhoff Publishers, 2011), 821–44.
van Harten, G., *Investment Treaty Arbitration and Public Law* (Oxford University Press, 2007).
Vasciannie, S., 'Bilateral Investment Treaties and Civil Strife: the AAPL/Sri Lanka Arbitration' *Netherlands Int. L. Rev.* 39 (1992) 333.
Virally, P., 'The Sources of International Law' in M. Sørensen (ed.), *Manual of Public International Law* (London: Macmillan, 1968).
Wälde, T., 'Confidential Awards as Precedent in Arbitration: Dynamics and Implication of Award Publication', in Gaillard and Banifatemi (eds.), *The Precedent in International Arbitration* 113.
Watts, A., 'Nationality of Claims: Some Relevant Concepts' in V. Lowe and M. Fitzmaurice (eds.), *Fifty Years of the International Court. Essays in Honor of Sir Robert Jennings* (Cambridge University Press, 1996), 432.
Weil, P., 'Cours général de droit international public' *Recueil des cours* 237 (1992).

Index

Index

Lightning Source UK Ltd.
Milton Keynes UK
UKHW022019090819
347738UK00010B/185/P

9 781107 022515